HOW TO START AND OPERATE YOUR OWN SUCCESSFUL OFFICE CLEANING BUSINESS

START, EXPAND AND DEVELOP YOUR OWN OFFICE CLEANING BUSINESS

JAMES REVIE

How to Start and Operate Your Own Successful Office Cleaning Business

Second Edition

Updated and expanded edition

Copyright © 2017 by James Revie

All rights reserved.

No part of this book may be reproduced in any form or by any electronic or mechanical means, including information storage and retrieval systems, without written permission from the author, except for the use of brief quotations in a book review.

CONTENTS

Acknowledgement	1
What Others Are Saying About	2
1. Introduction	5
2. Why the Cleaning Business?	10
3. A Short Testimony	13
4. Who Can Operate a Cleaning Business?	15
5. Getting Started	16
6. Equipment	22
7. Other Considerations	28
8. The Service Outline - Overview	33
9. How To Build Your Business For Profit	35
10. Practical Considerations	40
11. Marketing Strategies That Work - Part 1	42
12. The Appointment	50
13. Marketing Strategies That Work - Part 2	52
14. Hiring Workers	58
15. How To Price Offices For Profit	62
16. The Detailed Method Further Explained	68
17. How to Submit Your Quotation	71
18. How to Keep Your Contracts	75
19. About Your Telephone	76
20. How and When to Invoice	79
21. How to Clean Your Offices	81
22. Carpet Cleaning	92
23. Floor Care - Part 1	99
24. Floor Care - Part 2	106
25. How to Do Window Cleaning	118
26. How to Handle Complaints	121
27. Steps To Price Increases	123
28. Keys, Security and Alarm Systems	125
29. Selling Your Business	128
30. How To Deal With Taxes	130
31. How to Prepare the Service Outline	131
32. Viewing the Samples	138

33. How to Make Even More Money 145
34. Conclusion 147

HOW TO START AND OPERATE YOUR OWN SUCCESSFUL OFFICE CLEANING BUSINESS

ACKNOWLEDGEMENT

It is understood and acknowledged that this book is presented as information only. It is not a business plan, business advice or counseling advice in any way. The success referred to in this book in my/our own personal experience. Your's might vary. There are absolutely no warranties, liabilities or guarantees referred to, expected, implied or otherwise with regards to this book, the information therein and or the author(s), publisher(s) or agent(s).

WHAT OTHERS ARE SAYING ABOUT
HOW TO START & OPERATE YOUR OWN SUCCESSFUL OFFICE CLEANING BUSINESS

A complete explanation of the commercial cleaning industry...

I'm amazed at how much the the author was able to show without using video (although he makes t clear those are available as well). The included Service outline & service how-tos are well worth the nominal costs adapt them to fit your business & just get started. Everything you need to know is included in this book. By TAL

This book is absolutely fantastic...

This book is absolutely fantastic. A very easy to read and understand book that will motivate and inspire you to get going on starting your business as I am! Must buy!! By A_LEE22

Great Value for a Buck

This book covers all aspects of starting, operating, and selling a cleaning business "in detail". It addresses how to choose a Business Name, how to Register Your Business, setting up a Business Bank Account, obtaining Business Cards, obtaining Business Stationery, getting Business Insurance & Bonding, setting up your Office, the best ways to get Equipment & Supplies, how to get Contracts, how to Clean Office Spaces, and how to Sell The Business when you're ready. ByRobert Wilson

Cleaning

Very good book. Very straight forward and provided good steps to be taken from beginning to end. From how to start the company to getting the contract. By jones

Informative

This ebook was very informative and includes great examples of service outlines and advertising letters! I would highly recommend it if you are looking to start your cleaning business, as I am!

Surprisingly good

A surprisingly good book on this topic considering the price. ByBURT JACKSON

Easy reading and Lots of information!

I really enjoyed reading every second of this eBook, receiving knowledge from the author . It is very simple to read, everything is well explained. If you are planning on making a Cleaning business get this book, you won't regret it. Sample forms are very useful for the time you own your business. Contacting the author, James, is really simple and he will answer any question about the book. I definitely recommend this book. By Max Jon

Not bad for the price!

Very useful information from beginning to end. Would recommend to anyone needing to know about running their own business. Great job! Byjenn

Good for the money

Enjoyed this! Have already tried several of the straight forward marketing tips and can't say how confident I felt afterward. This is great edition to my business library.

By K. Barrantion

Great Outline for beginners and professionals

This ebook does a great job of outlining all the important facts about the cleaning business. Any questions u might have about cleaning offices for ex, how should I do this or that he explains it all. Thanks for the info. ByJoeon

Comprehensive and clear advice.

This book provides a well laid out and extremely detailed and comprehensive set of information and advice for those wanting to start, or improve a cleaning business. Absolutely recommended reading - good sound business advice all round. ByKim L

How to make money in the cleaning business

This is a great book full of references and valuable information. I recommend this book to anyone starting a home-based cleaning business. ByLoretta

1
INTRODUCTION

It is with great delight that I present to you this expanded Second Edition of **How To Start & Operate Your Own Successful Office Cleaning Business.**

Whatever your reason for reading this book I am convinced that this is the book for you. If you are a person who desires to change your financial future to an even more productive place, or if you want to provide for your family in a more powerful way or if you would like to make some very serious money, that is, full time income while only working part time - then this is the book for you.

This book is not just another book filled with fluffy generalizations about the Office Cleaning Business, but rather, it contains the methods and step by step explanation of what I have used for years to go from $0 per month to Thousands of dollars per month. I have explained in the chapter "Short Testimony" some of what the Office Cleaning Business has done for me and my family.

Although I can not guarantee your success, in any way, I can say that the easy methods that I have detailed in this book can be replicated by you. As I have made some serious monies - you can as well. You just need to know what the steps are and how to do them.

This book explains all of that, in a very clear no-fluff way.

This book is a written explanation of my own personal experiences of beginning and operating five successful cleaning business. You will get the benefit of my experience so you can apply these winning strategies to your own cleaning business.

Two of the greatest truths about this business is that you can start this business on a shoestring and you don't need any experience. You could actually start today and have money coming in very quickly.

During the 25 years of hands-on experience mentioned above, I have successfully learned how to start and operate cleaning businesses which include learning how to effectively acquire cleaning contracts, how to keep my customers happy and how to effectively price each of these contracts for a great profit. In addition, I have learned many easy and quick ways to do the various aspects of the business.

I have also learned that there are cleaning contracts that you will want to avoid while at the same time there will be contracts that you will want to acquire. The type of cleaning contracts you decide to service will make a huge difference to both your time and profits.

Within the pages of this book, you will discover how you to can obtain your own cleaning contracts, how to price them accurately and profitably, as well as, the key points in keeping your clients happy.

Furthermore, in this book, you will find a chapter that lists the types of contracts to avoid and the contracts that we have found to be the best to obtain. This information alone is more than worth the cost of this book in doing business the smart way.

You will discover that this book is not just a book of general ideas or theories, but rather it is a detailed book on the cleaning business giving you the exact step by step process that we have successfully put into practice to begin and operate your own money making office cleaning business.

You will be learning from someone who has been there and has the experience behind what is being said. I know what works and what doesn't work and have outlined all of this within the pages of this book.

That means that you don't have to do trial and error wondering and hoping if something will work or not. No more wasting time, energy and money. It is all laid out for you in this book. And if you have a question you can email directly for an answer.

In a later chapter, you will learn the step by step cleaning business system that we have developed regarding the actual operation of the cleaning business and in particular regarding the various cleaning duties. This easy to follow system will save you time, money and frustration. This proven system will allow you to get in and out of a client's office quickly and have very happy clients because of the quality of your service.

There are easy ways to operate a cleaning business and there are hard ways. Within the pages of this book, we will show you the easy ways of doing business. There is no need for you to re-invent the wheel. Why not take full advantage of our experience. We will show you what we have learned.

You will also find in the following chapters a few links for video illustrations of various cleaning steps which will allow you to actually see these steps in action.

Regarding the topic of obtaining cleaning contracts, I have actually had people come to me, who were already in the cleaning business, and ask me to obtain cleaning contracts for them. They offered to pay me a fee to do this. I didn't do it because I was only interested in operating my own business. However, these methods that those people were willing to pay for is fully revealed and explained in detail in this book for you.

As mentioned above, there are many types of cleaning contracts to consider, but over the years and through the "school of hard knocks" we have discovered the best contracts to obtain - that is - the best contracts that will allow you to do the job at minimal cost and highest profit.

I want to pass this information to you so you can benefit from what I have learned. The principles in this book will save you time and allow you to make money faster.

Over the years I have had the opportunity of building several successful cleaning businesses from scratch, obtain the cleaning contracts, hire employees as needed, work with managers and corporate VIPs, and train other people just starting out and those who are also in the cleaning business in actually how to do the cleaning business successfully.

All of this and more I will show you in this book. You will have inside information from someone who has been there and has successfully done it - over and over again.

Also, in this book I have include what I call the "Service Outline" agreement. This is a fully Ready Made written presentation/agreement that you will give to you prospective clients. When preparing this Service Outline, and we show you step by step how to do this, you just need to put in your details and it is ready to go.

We call this Service Outline one of our little gems. This little gem is worth its weight in gold. In the chapter that deals with the "Service Outline", I will show you how to easily use it. You will discover why it is so valuable and profitable to you. This "Service Outline" will make it easier to avoid any confusion as to what you have agreed to do for your client and promote great client relationships and communication.

This "Service Outline" has been a great tool for us. It is such a great tool that others have tried to copy or steal our "Service Outline" for their own use. The "Service Outline" is included in this book for you to use as a tool for your own cleaning business.

There is so much more for you to know beyond what I have briefly stated above. Have a quick look at the Table Of Contents and see for yourself all the areas that this book will cover.

Please note that in this book the terms "Cleaning Business", "Office Cleaning Business" and "Janitorial Business" are used interchangeably.

2

WHY THE CLEANING BUSINESS?

In today's sagging economy where people are losing their jobs and our dollar seems to be losing its value, the type of business that will excel and continue to grow and prosper will be the **service type business**. The Cleaning Business is an excellent service type business.

No matter how bad the economy gets there will be businesses that will require their offices to be cleaned. Doctors and Lawyers are not going to dust their own desks and empty their own trash cans. Engineers are not going to wash their own floors and vacuum their carpets. But they will pay you very handsomely for doing it for them.

Actually, in so many cases, we found that we were making more money cleaning offices than the bosses who hired us were making themselves. I remember reading a testimony of a young man who graduated from University as a CPA. After a short period of time he realized that he could make more money providing Office Cleaning Services to others - than he would be able to make in his Accounting career.

For whatever reasons you want to or need to make some serious money, we have found the Cleaning Business was the answer. Because we did it - there should be no reason why you can't do it also.

One of the great benefits of the Office Cleaning Business is that you do not have all your income based on one client. All of your eggs will not be in one basket as the saying goes. Your income is spread over a number of different clients. Therefore, if one of your clients goes under - you don't.

Instead you continue to grow your business (and bank account) by acquiring new clients, by using the principles set out in this book. And again, these are the same principles that we have used for years.

The economy doesn't affect you as much as it would if you only had one source of income. Some people in the Cleaning Business would even go as far as to say that the Cleaning Business is about the only "recession proof" business there is.

Another benefit of this great business is that you can make your cleaning business as small or as big as you want. It is in your own hands. You decide what you want to do. I know of some people that have kept it small. They work at it part time. This allows them to obtain some of the nice things in life that they wouldn't otherwise have. While other people have built their cleaning business to the point that they can "fire their boss" and experience financial freedom, working their own hours and being their own boss.

And yet there are others who have built their cleaning business to a large size and expanded into neighboring towns or cities with a large number of clients. The choice is yours as to what you desire to do. Whatever your decision, you will find this book to be a powerful information tool.

When it comes to the competition in the Cleaning Business, we found that competition didn't really matter. By using the easy strategies explained in this book we were able to completely bypass and competition and deal directly with the decision makers in each office.

We found that it really didn't matter how many other janitorial companies were in our city we were able to grow our business successfully. These are some of the strategies you will learn in this book so you can have a growing successful cleaning business

By the way, we don't even use "Yellow Page display advertising". Instead we use the same principles outlined in this book to obtain and keep our clients. In the past we have tried Yellow Book display advertising only to find out that it really didn't pay. It is good, however, to have a single line advertisement in the white pages. Some telephone companies will give you a single line Yellow Page advertisement for a very reasonable cost. This is also good to consider.

This will allow any prospective customers - who chooses to look you up in the Yellow pages - the opportunity to see you there. We have discovered that you don't need to spend hundreds of dollars per month on a fancy telephone book advertisement. We didn't - we just used the information and principles that I have outlined in this book.

3
A SHORT TESTIMONY

What has the cleaning business done for us? Over the years the cleaning business has provided the means by which we could purchase several rental properties as investments, purchase 10 acres of land, build a custom built home and purchase several vehicles.

Two of my family members decided they would like to go to college; so our entire family picked up and moved our entire household across the country to the West Coast and established a home there. Before we moved, we sold our already established cleaning business for a great profit, trained the new owners in all the principles found in this eBook and used that money to move and get established on the West Coast.

When we arrived on the West Coast, I soon started a new cleaning business, using the same principles outlined in this eBook. This cleaning business was to completely support our family - and it did. We were able to purchase all that was needed to set up a home in a new location - including purchasing two vehicles. This also included financing the tuition for three years for those two family members, purchasing of books and supplies - in addition to what I have stated above. As you may know, College is not cheap and this was for two family members, not just one.

Our cleaning business worked out so well on the West Coast that we actually divided the business into two separate profitable cleaning businesses.

After these two family members had completed their studies, our family again picked up stakes and moved back home. This required setting up home again and yes, starting another successful cleaning business from scratch. It all worked out beautifully.

I will also say at this point that we also believe in the power of prayer and the favor of God. Although we were operating a great business we attribute its success to answered prayer and God's favor.

4

WHO CAN OPERATE A CLEANING BUSINESS?

If you can vacuum a carpet and dust a desk, you can do office cleaning. Or if you can handle people and have someone who can do the cleaning for you, again, you can do office cleaning.

The cleaning business is very versatile. After obtaining a cleaning contract, if for some reason you dislike it, you can cancel your services and obtain other contracts more to your liking. The cleaning business is also perhaps the easiest and most stable business to get into. In addition, the cleaning business does not require large sums of investment capital or years of college education in order to make it successful.

With the information contained in this book, together with your own common sense, you should be able to start your own profitable cleaning business.

Remember that this is not a get rich quick scheme that will rake in millions overnight. It will take effort and time on your part.

5

GETTING STARTED

In this section we will cover a number of fundamental, but essential areas. These areas include: setting up your home office, office stationery, work space, your business name your telephone, insurance and other important topics. These areas are essential to the smooth running of your business. Should you already have experience and are thus "well versed" in the areas discussed in this chapter, please feel free to skip this section and move onto the next section.

A Business Name

Before you begin your cleaning business you must choose a business name. You can use your own name, or you may prefer to use any name that comes to mind that portrays the Janitorial cleaning business. Some husband and wife teams use the first initial of their names for a business name. For example: J.R. Cleaning Services or W.F. Building Maintenance.

One consideration to keep in mind is that if you decide to sell your cleaning business later, if you have chosen to name your business using your own personal name, you may not want someone else using your name. We have used our own name in the past, but have found it best to use a name that does not contain your personal or family name. Check the Yellow Pages and White Pages of your phone book to see what other cleaning services are calling themselves.

Registering Your Business

After choosing a name you will want to register your business with your state or province. This will make sure that someone else doesn't steal or use your business name. Each province or state is different and has its own registration forms for registering a business. These forms are usually readily available from any government office or law office, usually free of charge and take only a few minutes to fill out. We found that we didn't need a lawyer to do this. We just filled in the forms and mailed them with the required fee to the government address listed on the form.

Business Bank Account

You will need to establish a business checking account at your local bank. Since you will be invoicing your clients using your business name, your clients in turn will be making checks payable to your company name; thus, a business checking account is necessary. We will provide you with a sample invoice further on in this book. Feel free to change it to reflect your own information and freely use it.

If you're happy with the bank you're presently dealing with, open a business checking account there. There will be a few forms to complete, but the bank will complete them with and for you.

Business Cards

The next consideration is that of business cards. This will be one of the most important assets of your business. When you are speaking to prospective clients more than likely they will ask for your business card. It can be embarrassing and unprofessional if you do not have any.

You don't need to spend a lot of money on business cards. A plain, clean looking, and inexpensive card that gives your company name, your name, address and phone number is all that is necessary.

With today's computers and printers and the available tear-off printable cards available from most stationery stores, it makes printing your own sharp looking business cards a snap. If you use Word Perfect or MS Word and have a color or black printer or even a laser printer, you can design and make your own professional looking business cards.

Visit your local business stationery store and pick out a pre-printed design that you like. Avery Labels provides the tear-off printable cards and even provides software to design and print your own cards. Many stationery stores sell Avery Business Cards, but you can also order them online. View Avery's website at http://www.avery.com. Also, Staples can provide a selection of cards as well. See http://www.staples.com

The cost will vary, but will be approximately $6 - 7 for approximately 250 cards. These prices may vary from location to location. These pre-printed designed cards are usually 10 on a sheet and come in various designs and colors. All you have to do is add the details of your business using the software mentioned above and then print them to complete a great looking card.

An alternative that you may wish to consider is having your business cards printed through Vista Print (http://www.vistaprint.com). They provide a variety of sample cards to consider. Their prices vary to whatever you would like to pay. I have seen some advertising from them that they also offer a selection of free business cards. You just pay for the shipping.

The one advantage of this method is that you don't have to do the design and printing. You just fill out the online forms at Vista Print, pay for them by credit card and they will arrive within a short time. I have seen their work and it is very nicely done.

Business Stationery

Business stationery need not be elaborate. A simple letterhead that can also be used as an invoice is all you need. Just as with business cards, you can either have a company print your letterheads for you or you can do them yourself.

The easiest way we have found is to make our own letterhead. There really is no need to go out and spend money to have someone do it for you unless you really want to do this. We simply use WordPerfect or MS Word and design our own. We keep it simple, professional looking and clean.

If you don't have WordPerfect or MS Word then basically any Windows or Mac based word processor will do. These programs will usually have what is called scalable fonts so you can make letters and words bigger or smaller as you desire. If you do not have a good word processor and would like a free one that is MS Word compatible you can go to Open Office at http://www.openoffice.org They have a version for most computing platforms - Windows, Mac, and Linux.

If you decide you would like to have a little fancier letterhead and invoice then you could also go the route of purchasing pre-printed designer letterheads from your local stationery store such as Staples or Walmart. We have included a sample letterhead and invoice in this book so you can see what it would look like.

Business Insurance/Liability

Business insurance is something that you should also consider at some point. There are basically two types of insurance to examine. The first is liability insurance and the second is bonding.

Here would be an example of the need for liability insurance; if someone comes into the office that you are cleaning, slips on the wet floor and injures himself – then you would need liability insurance. This insurance will cover the other person's injuries.

Of course, if you are washing a floor in a public area while the business office is still open, and people are coming in and out, you will be wise to use a sign indicating that the floor is wet - thus protecting yourself. These signs are of the plastic "A" frame type and can be obtained from your local janitorial supply house.

However, the type of cleaning that we do is after hours - when the office is closed and nobody is around. Thus the possibility of someone getting hurt by slipping on a wet floor or whatever is greatly reduced. However this same liability is still something to consider and some clients may ask you if you have it.

Bonding

Bonding is another consideration. A Fidelity bond or an Honesty bond is a bond that is provided by an insurance company that will cover a predetermined amount of possible loss to your client in the event of theft. The amount can range from $5,000 and up.

Basically, the bottom line is that bonding gives your client assurance of your honesty. And in the event that they suffer loss, they have recourse to recover any loss they think they might have. Shop around for bonding insurance.

Different companies charge different rates. Don't just accept the first rate you are quoted. Our policy has been to obtain at least three quotes. If you have a good insurance agent (perhaps for your house or car) you may wish to contact him/her. If not, just take a stroll in the Yellow Pages and obtain your three quotes.

Your Office

In the cleaning business you do not need a fancy office as such. You can use a room in your home as an office. A spare room or even a part of a room is great. A room in your basement, with a desk, a telephone, and a filing cabinet or some means of holding files is all you need. There is no need for you to go out and rent office space. This would be a needless expense.

If you use a part of your home, depending on which country you live in, this could be a great tax deduction for you at income tax time. Closer to the time of filing your tax return you can obtain information about various deductions that may be available to you.

If you need space to store your equipment and supplies, perhaps a spot in the garage, in the basement or even a spare room can be utilized to store your cleaning equipment when not in use.

Another consideration for storage space is that some of the offices you will be cleaning may have a Janitor's room or similar storage room that is big enough to store janitorial equipment.

Transportation

Transportation is not a big problem. The vehicle you have is all you need for now. The equipment you will need for nightly cleaning will be a dust mop, vacuum cleaner, a dusting pail containing dusters, window cleaner, etc., and a deck or yacht mop. All of these should easily fit into the trunk of a domestic or even some foreign cars.

6

EQUIPMENT

Somewhere along the line you will need some cleaning equipment. If you can afford to buy the equipment up front that's good. If not, don't worry about it. You probably have most of the equipment you need in your own home.

Most people have a good working vacuum cleaner, as well as dusters, cleanser, sponges and the like. Below are some guidelines that will help you in selecting the equipment you need.

Vacuum Cleaner

Don't make the mistake of going out and purchasing an expensive sophisticated buffing machine or an expensive do-all vacuum cleaner. Eventually you will need a floor buffing machine and a good vacuum cleaner.

Just buy what you need and only when you need it. And buy only what you need, not something with a lot of bells and whistles that only looks impressive. Your first couple of cleaning contracts might be totally carpeted offices and a floor machine may not be needed - so why buy one until you need one?

Usually every home has a vacuum cleaner of some sort. If your vacuum cleaner works well then use it for now. However, later when the need arises you will want to purchase a good commercial vacuum cleaner.

There are many vacuum cleaners on the market today and we have tried many, many of these different makes. But the vacuum cleaners that we have found to be the best for the Commercial Cleaning industry are the Eureka Commercial upright vacuum and the Sanitaire Vacuum.

If you decide to purchase a new vacuum cleaner, a great vacuum to consider is Sanitaire Vacuums. We have found them to be absolutely excellent. They work well and are easy to repair (belts, etc.) and last a long time. They go the distance in terms of usability.

Here is a link to a company that sells Sanitaire Vacuums online. http://www.sanitairevac.com/ Also, here is link from Amazon on the Sanitaire Vacuums they sell. https://goo.gl/ac9w8s. Just type these link addresses into your favorite browser.

If you would like to find other dealers for Sanitaire Vacuums you can just Google "Sanitaire Vacuums" and this will provide several listings for you.

Over the years vacuum cleaners have improved greatly and have also come down in price. Whatever vacuum you choose, be sure to get one that uses a "HEPA" filter. This can be a great selling point when you are speaking with a prospective client.

With regards to commercial vacuums, they come in various sizes: 12-13 inch (regular) and 15-16 inch (wide track). The size of the track depends on the manufacturer. Actually, there are some Commercial Vacuums that have an even wider track, but for the purposes of this book we will just use the two example widths.

Unless you have a lot of carpet to vacuum, the regular 12 inch model will do. We have had the 12 inch, 16 inch and the 24 inch. We found the standard 12 inch was the best for maneuvering around desks and other office furniture.

If you have people working for you, you will also want to provide them with a vacuum cleaner that will not be heavy in terms of weight. A wider vacuum tends to be heavier and more difficult to maneuver and therefore will generally take longer to vacuum an office.

Make sure that the Eureka vacuum or whichever vacuum you choose is at least a 6.5 amp motor rating - as indicated on the ID plate under the vacuum. Anything less than this rating we have found will not last under heavy commercial use.

Most of the newer vacuum cleaners today have a motor rating anywhere from 6.5 to 10 amps. However, if the amount of carpet that you need to vacuum is very small, like an entrance mat or just one office room then you can use a vacuum with less than a 6.5 rating with success.

One thing to keep in mind when you are selecting a vacuum is that when you clean your client's office you will be plugging the vacuum into one of their standard electrical outlets. Usually, as we have found, many offices have many other things plugged into the same outlets or on the same circuit breaker. If you use a vacuum that is, say rated at 12-15 amps, you could blow the fuse or trip the circuit breaker. Therefore, using a lower powered vacuum is always a good thing to consider.

Also make sure that the vacuum you choose has a HEPA filter system with either an additional filter bag or cup that empties the dirt out. We moved away from the old vinyl bags years ago because we found them to be not as sanitary as the newer HEPA systems. The more you can filter the air going in and out the better for total cleanliness.

Now you do not have to buy your vacuum new. If you check around the different vacuum supply stores or Janitorial Supply houses, or even check your newspaper, you may be able to pick up a good used Eureka or Sanitaire vacuum at a very reasonable price.

When considering a used vacuum, make sure that it runs quietly: not with a whirring or grinding sound - indicating a defective bearing. And also make sure that there are no cracks or holes in the base of the vacuum cleaner.

However, if you buy a used vacuum from a Janitorial Supply house they usually test and overhaul their vacuums to insure that they are in good condition. You can find your local Janitorial Supply house by simply looking in your Yellow Pages under "Janitorial Supplies".

You should expect to pay anywhere from $15 to $200 for a good used commercial vacuum. They are about $190.00 and up new. Don't hold me to these prices as they could vary from city to city and from state to state.

Floor Machines

Buy New, Used or Rent?

A floor machine is another piece of equipment that you will need in your cleaning business at some point. But again, do not go out and buy one until you need it. And don't buy the best or most expensive one available – it's not necessary.

You can also buy them used. In the startup of your business you may not even need one because your client's offices might be totally carpeted with only a small front entrance to mop. Later in this book I will show you which offices are the easiest to maintain with the least amount of effort.

If you don't want to buy a buffing/stripping machine you can rent one from a rental company. There are a number of cleaning businesses that do that.

A floor machine or floor buffer/stripper as some call it is used to polish and or strip floors. Later in this book I will explain how to buff and strip a floor like a professional. Remember, when the time comes that you need a floor machine you can either purchase a used or new one or you could even rent one as you need it.

If you wish to purchase a used floor machine you can check your local newspaper or Janitorial Supply house for one. You may even want to run a small classified ad in your local newspaper indicating your interest in buying used Janitorial equipment. We have done this with good results.

Also, some larger cleaning companies will sell their used equipment for a good price. We have also found some good deals by purchasing some equipment from leasing companies that lease Janitorial equipment to other cleaning companies. When their lease is up, the equipment often comes available for purchase. These machines could be purchased through the leasing company. There are various kinds of floor machines available: from regular low speed machines to high speed machines and even ultra-high speed burnishing machines.

We will discuss floor machines in more detail a little later in this book. The low speed machines are good for stripping and scrubbing floors. They do the hard work for you. The high speed machines are good for general floor spray buffing. While the ultra-high speed burnishing machines are for very high traffic areas and are used in areas like supermarkets, malls, etc. We will explain how to strip, scrub and buff a floor further in this book.

In our experience, we have been very selective as to the types of offices we would clean. This made the amount of equipment needed minimal and the profits larger. In this book I will explain this "selection of offices" in more detail for you.

Someone has said that when it comes to understanding what a floor machine looks like that it looks basically similar to a household floor buffer. However, a commercial floor machine will be larger, weigh more and have only one rubber drive pad. Underneath the drive pad colored pads will be placed. The color of the pad will determine what function the floor machine will perform. For instance, a white or red buffing pad will buff the floors while a green or black pad (much coarser) will scrub or strip the floor. I will explain how this is done in detail as we go through this book.

The speed at which the floor machine rotates is important. Low speed machines rotate at about 175 rpm, while high speed machines rotate around 300-450 rpm and ultra-high speeds anywhere up to 2000 rpm. If you have a large area of floor space to clean/polish, the higher speed machines get you through the job faster.

The ultra-high speed machine is also called a Burnisher and is generally used in large areas such as a supermarket, large grocery stores or shopping mall. However, for all intents and purposes the machine you will be looking for to start with will be a **LOWER SPEED MACHINE.**

7

OTHER CONSIDERATIONS
DUST MOPS AND DUSTERS

Other items that you will need in your cleaning business will be a wash mop, pail and wringer. The pail and wringer can be purchased new or even used if you wish, very inexpensively through the similar sources as mentioned above. When obtaining a wash mop, usually a 16 oz. string mop will meet the need. The cotton mops are less expensive, but the Rayon mop heads will last longer.

Also, you will need a dust mop: like a household dust mop, but only wider. A dust mop is used to sweep uncarpeted floors - tiled, terrazzo etc.

Using a dust mop rather than a conventional brush type broom is faster and prevents dust getting into the air while sweeping. When you are cleaning an office you will want to keep the dust level down as much as possible while at the same time using equipment that will get you in and out quickly.

Get a standard 24 inch treated dust mop. This is what we use. They are treated with a dust magnet chemical to attract dust and hold it while you sweep the floor. You can obtain your dust mop and the dust magnet chemical from a local Janitorial supply house at a very reasonable cost. However, we have found it more advantageous to rent both our dust mops and dusting cloths from a dust control rental company.

Usually uniform rental companies or those who rent walkway mats (the kind that Banks use at their front entrances) also rent dust mops and dusters. Renting dust mops and dusters provides us with a tax deduction and always assures us of clean dust mops and dusters.

We have paid about as little as $2.20/month/per dust mop. The company we use picks them up, cleans them, treats them and then returns them to us. And for $.25 per duster/per month they pick them up, clean them and return them to us as well.

This has been a tremendous time saver for us because it saves us the hassle of trying to always be on the lookout for a supply of dusters. Whichever company you may use might also charge you a small flat rate fee as an energy/fuel cost fee, but this is much easier than trying to clean them and treat them yourself.

Costs will vary according to your location. Just check in the "Yellow Pages" under either "Duster Rentals", "Uniform Rentals", or "Walkway Mat Rentals". As mentioned above, usually the company that carries these items will also carry the dust mop and dusters.

If you decide not to go the dust mop rental avenue and rather purchase your dust mop(s) directly from a Janitorial Supply house, it is vitally important that you also use a commercial Janitorial grade dust mop treating chemical.

We have, in the past, tried using dust magnet chemicals available at the local supermarket only to find out the floors ended up being slippery and over a period of time required more maintenance. We have found that it has saved us time and money using the proper commercial chemicals.

If you choose to go the route of renting your dusters from a rental company - as mentioned above - it is vitally important that you rent the "White lint free" dusters. Some companies cater to both Janitorial and Auto services. You will not want to use the typical "blue" hand wipes that are used in auto repair shops.

The white lint free dusters are not generally used in auto shops and therefore there is almost no chance of getting dusters with grease or automotive oil on them which could be transferred to your client's desk or cabinets.

So, as I have already mentioned, even though the duster company cleans the blue duster/wipes they will not guarantee that there wouldn't be stains on them. It is best to stick with the "White lint free" dusters that are not used in the auto industry. These are the same kinds that are sometimes used in fine furniture stores.

Miscellaneous

You will also need a can of cleanser such as Ajax, Comet or similar, a sponge for cleaning sinks, a container of glass cleaner, a container of general purpose liquid cleaner, a container of floor finish (more on this later) and some 26X36 garbage bags. For general purposes you can purchase the cheapest kind found in the grocery store. Buy the cleanser and glass cleaner from your local supermarket when on sale. It will probably be cheaper than the Janitorial supply house.

The general purpose cleaner is used for general washing of tile, terrazzo and brick floors as found in front entrances, bathrooms etc. It can also be used to wash floors that have been finished with a floor finish. Finger prints and scuff marks on walls, doors etc. can be removed by using a general purpose cleaner and in some cases by using a glass cleaner.

We have found that the best kind of general purpose cleaner is what is called a "non-scum" general purpose cleaner. If you are washing polished/buffed floors such as tiles, terrazzo, marble etc. this kind of cleaner will not leave a dull film on the floor.

A dull film left on the floor will spoil the good look of the floor and will also show what we call "rub off" marks as people rub off the film on the floor as they walk on it. When this "rub off" happens it makes the floor look like it hasn't been professionally taken care of. A "non scum" cleaner takes care of this beautifully.

Floor finish or floor wax as some call it, is needed to refinish a freshly stripped floor. It is also used in re-coating and spray buffing. This will be explained in more detail as we continue in this book. The general purpose "non scum" cleaner and the floor finish can be purchased from your local Janitorial supply house. Just buy them as you need them.

If you don't need a lot of garbage bags, they can be bought from the local supermarket. However; on the other hand, if you feel you'll need more than just a handful of garbage bags check out your local Janitorial supply house for the best prices. They sell the garbage bags usually in boxes of about 250. If you are starting up on a shoe string then you only need to buy a couple of packages of garbage bags from your local supermarket.

Keep in mind that for general garbage, garbage bags don't need to be the toughest, best, and thickest. Just get the least expensive. One exception to this would be if you are cleaning banks.

Many banks require their garbage to be kept in their basement or storage room for a period of anywhere from a week to two weeks. This is just in case they have made an error and need to search through the garbage to find a receipt or some document. If there is a possibility that they will be going through multiple garbage bags looking for something - then garbage bags that are a little heavier would be to your advantage.

We have found that banks do indeed do this and heavier bags have been a blessing. Again, the idea is to save yourself some time by being able to get in and get out quickly.

So..... How are you doing???

Feeling a little overwhelmed? Well don't worry. It seems like a lot but really it isn't. Just go over it slowly and don't rush it. It really is much easier than what it may seem at first. When you look back on all of this you will realize that it really is quite easy.

Again, as I have mentioned before, we will look with more detail at some of the items above a little later in this eBook.

Let's continue now and briefly look at what is called the Service Outline. This is a very important part of your business. We will discuss the Service Outline in detail a little later near the end of this book. But for now let's just see what it is all about.

8

THE SERVICE OUTLINE - OVERVIEW

In this chapter we will look at a brief overview of the Service Outline. We have provided a chapter that will deal with the actual "How To Prepare The Service Outline" in detail, further in this book. But let's get started with this overview.

When you approach a prospective client to clean their office, it is very important that you put down in writing what you will do for them as their cleaning company. Your clients will expect this and will be looking for it. This is where you will give them an "Outline" of the services you will provide.

We have enclosed a sample Service Outline for you. You do not need to go to any great expense in order to use it. All you will have to do is have whatever company name you have chosen, together with your address and phone number placed at the top of the outline and your company name placed on the last line of the outline and then simply photocopy the rest. This is the easiest, the best and the cheapest way to go.

Another way of preparing your Service Outline is to have the outline on your computer and just fill in the required areas with the information that pertains to your client. This is a very quick and easy way of doing it. Preparing the outline in this fashion will allow you to present a very personalized outline with your client's name and all of the areas of servicing that you intend to do.

The outline enclosed is the actual outline that we have used for years. The only difference is that we have our outline on computer, as mentioned above, and print each outline as required. We will discuss the "Outline" in detail with you a little later in this eBook.

The outline has been carefully drawn up to both include all the necessary items that prospective customers would consider important and to exclude any unnecessary items.

NOTE: The outline that we have enclosed is alone worth more than the price of the book itself. This outline has been a tremendous success for us for years.

9

HOW TO BUILD YOUR BUSINESS FOR PROFIT
WITH THE BEST CONTRACTS

In our next chapter we will be looking at the topic of marketing your cleaning business. But before we get to that, it is important to first discuss what **types** of cleaning contracts we have found to be the best and why.

This is a very important chapter and I would highly recommend that you read it at least twice so you will have e a good grasp of the principles explained.

Types of Contracts To Consider

We have found over the years that there are specific cleaning contracts that we would avoid like the plague, while, at the same time, there were clients we would pursue.

In the cleaning business the possibilities as to the types of cleaning contracts available are almost endless.

These general possibilities could include:

- Restaurants

- Oil companies
- Auto dealerships
- Bus companies
- Parts dealerships
- Tar and petroleum bi-product companies
- General stores
- Doctors' offices
- Banks
- Finance companies
- Schools
- Lawyers' offices
- General commercial type offices, etc.

This is only a small sampling of the vastness of what is available.

However, it will be very beneficial for you to know that the **type of cleaning contracts** you choose to service will **make all the difference** in the world to you and your business in terms of time, labor and profit.

Over the years, we have cleaned just about every contract type you could imagine. However, we have learned that the best way to build our business was to service what is called Professional Offices. These types of contracts would be easy to clean, require the least amount of equipment, labor and time to service.

This type of cleaning is <u>not</u> Industrial, Institutional or Biological, but **Professional Office Cleaning.** We have found that there is a huge difference in every respect, including profitability.

When we say, "Professional Office Cleaning" we mean the cleaning of:

- Lawyers' offices
- Accountants' offices
- Investment companies
- Paper products companies
- Brick manufacturing companies (offices only)
- Plumbing and electrical companies (offices only)
- Insurance companies
- Banks
- Finance companies
- General "professional" offices
- And other offices that would easily fit into this list

Here's the bottom line: you want professional offices that do not have oil and grease being tracked through the office area. You want offices that are easy to clean, require little equipment and that can be cleaned quickly with great results so that your client is kept happy for years to come while you make a great profit.

Please don't misunderstand what I am saying here. If you desire to accept every contract type that comes your way that is just fine. However, what we have learned over the years is the most profitable and best contracts for us to service are the ones I've just mentioned above.

With this type of clientele, you go in after hours - when there is no one around and just do your work. As long as you provide a great service, you will get paid each and every month just like clockwork. In some ways, it's almost like a guaranteed income that you can increase anytime you want by simply obtaining more contracts.

It's just like giving yourself a raise anytime you want!

Size of Contracts to Consider

Not only does the type of contract you consider make a difference, but the size of the contract is also important.

There are many opportunities in the cleaning business to bid on many different sizes of contracts. The size of the contract you will go after is totally your own decision. In our own cleaning business we have serviced a wide variety of office sizes.

However, we have found over the years that smaller offices are the most profitable and easiest to clean. Again, when I say "easiest to clean" this is with the understanding of the "types" of contracts that I have mentioned above.

In our own experience we have found the best contracts to obtain are smaller size offices. The model of office cleaning that we practiced was to obtain smaller contracts that require little cleaning in which we could be in and out quickly and provide great results for our clients. The amount that we could charge for this type of office cleaning was very rewarding and provided us with a great profit margin.

We will discuss the three methods of pricing a cleaning contract a little later in this book.

The size of the offices that we would service would range from a small once per week office that would take about 20-30 minutes per cleaning to offices (5 nights per week) around the 20,000 square foot size.

The offices that we cleaned once per week and that took about 20-30 minutes per cleaning averaged about $100 per hour. While servicing the larger offices we still made some serious monies, but not as much as we did with the smaller offices.

I am not suggesting you charge $100 per hour. I cannot tell you how much to charge. You will need to take into consideration such variables as where you live and the standard rate in your state/province in order to arrive at an appropriate price. But you can charge a higher amount per cleaning if the contract is once or twice a week as compared to 5 nights per week. We have explained the reasons for this in another chapter.

As already mentioned, we have provided you with the three methods that we ourselves use to price offices. You can use these very same methods in your own business.

Again, in our own business we built up a route of these types of offices (well paying, easy to clean) and systematically serviced them according to the needed frequency of cleaning. We made some serious money in our business as you can read in the chapter called, "A Short Testimony".

At the end of the day the size and type of offices you decide to service will be your own choice. The information in this book will help you in whatever direction you have chosen.

10

PRACTICAL CONSIDERATIONS
HOW TO PICK THE BEST OFFICES

We have already touched on the topic of "Types" of contracts in the previous chapter. In this chapter I want to give you further details with some **real life** practical examples that I think will help you and allow you to see a bigger picture.

When you tour an office, it is important for you to notice how dirty and congested the office is as well as the type of business your prospective clients are involved in. This will help you in your pricing. This will also help you decide if you actually even want to clean their offices in the first place.

For example - when we cleaned an oil company that had wall to wall light blue carpeting in the offices, we discovered that the workers would track the oil into the office and the carpet would become oil covered. This of course would necessitate continual steam cleaning. We did this and charged the company more money for doing it.

However, we found that when weighing the amount of time required in terms of scheduling and staffing with the amount of money gained, that at the end of the day, it was much better to obtain a contract that would pay multiple amounts more than the extra fees we would charge.

In another situation we cleaned a tar company and again, the workers would track the tar into the main and side offices (ceramic tiled floors) and this required continuous weekly scrubbing of the floors with harsh and dangerous chemicals to remove the tar from the floors.

Again, we charged more money, but over time found that it wasn't worth it. So we obtained contracts that paid more money, were much easier to clean and didn't have the problem of either oil or tar being tracked in.

Giving you the above examples is only to share with you the experience of a person who has spent years in the cleaning business and knows which types of offices are easy to clean, more profitable and desirable to obtain as compared to the cleaning contracts to avoid.

The cleaning business is an absolutely great profitable and easy to do business. The cleaning business can be either part time or full time. The choice is totally yours.

The great thing about having your own cleaning business is that because you are your own boss, you can be "picky" about the type of cleaning contracts you will clean and the types you won't clean.

11

MARKETING STRATEGIES THAT WORK - PART 1

HOW TO GET CONTRACTS

In order to obtain clients you, of course, need to let them know about your services. You will need to market your cleaning services. This is not really difficult and we will show how we have done it successfully.

There are many different ways to do this and only your own imagination will limit the ways. Below we will look at a number of ways in which we have successfully marketed our cleaning services to prospective clients. As already mentioned the methods below are the tried, true and proven methods we have used for successfully for years.

Method 1.

One method is to just walk into an office that you would like to clean and ask directly for the manager. When he arrives on the scene you can hand him your card and/or advertising letter, briefly tell him who you are and your interest in cleaning his office, and that you would be delighted to give him a free quotation. Do not push it at this point, but let it rest with him - you can always get back to him again.

If the manager is tied up or not available you can leave a sealed advertising letter with his name on it with the receptionist. The reason the advertising letter should be sealed is because the receptionist may take it upon herself to decide for the manager whether they need new cleaners or not and so in deciding may throw out your letter and you will be short circuited.

We have gained business this way - by simply delivering, by hand, handbills (sealed advertising letters) to different offices that we really wanted to clean. We either walked in and presented the letter to the receptionist or dropped it in the "mail" slot after they were closed. At the end of this book is a copy of two sample advertising letters we have used with great results. Please feel free to use them for your own cleaning business purposes.

Keep in mind that this method works well with small offices like insurance offices, lawyer's offices and finance companies. However, larger offices require a different approach as explained below.

Method 2.

Another method that we have found very effective is to obtain a list of the businesses in your town and send them an advertising letter directly. This list can be obtained easily from your "Yellow Pages" or a commercial directory book listing businesses in your area. Usually libraries carry different business directories and lists of businesses. Also your local government economic commission or economic development department may also carry a list of businesses in your area.

The information from the library is easy to obtain and is free. Many of these lists from whichever source you choose come complete with the company's name, address, phone number, fax number and usually the owner's name with the list of officers; including the purchasing manager's name. With this list you can address envelopes directly to the person in charge of the company that you desire to do business with.

We have also found it a great success to drive around the area or Commercial Park where many commercial offices are located and write down the names of the companies and the address of each. Then we used this list to send direct advertising letters to them in the mail.

The person you will address will be the "Purchasing Manager" or "Office Manager". The person you will want to contact will be the person who is able to make the decision about hiring your company. If you have all the information on the company but not the person's name to contact, you can either call the company and ask for his name, or send the advertising letter and put under the last line of the address the words "ATT: Purchasing Manager". We have done this with good success.

NOTE: We have found that in smaller offices the person to contact would be the "Office Manager". However, in larger corporate offices the person would be the "Purchasing Manager". Someone might ask "what kind of response would you get from this method?" In our own personal experience we have found that the response of this method can range from 3-5%. This response makes the cost of envelopes and stamps very worthwhile.

Method 3.

The **least expensive** and **most effective** method of contacting clients that we have used is by obtaining the list of businesses described in method 2, calling them directly on the phone, asking for the "Purchasing Manager" and then explaining our services to him directly.

Below I have included a "telephone presentation." Just write it out and practice it on your family. If you use this method, when you call your prospective clients you will have everything right in front of you. The worst thing that could happen is that he will say, "Thank You, but I'm not interested."

Knowing When to Call

Knowing what day of the week to call is very important. We have found that Mondays and Fridays were poor days to call. When the manager comes in on Mondays he is busy getting over the weekend that he's just had and trying to get back into the work mode. Many executives use Monday as a catch up day or a planning day for the rest of the week. While others use this day as a day to try to get finished with as little as possible out of the ordinary.

On Friday he is more interested in getting through the day and getting into his weekend. Over and over again we have found Tuesday, Wednesday or Thursday the best days to call.

Most listings of businesses will give you the owner's name and also the names of the officers of the company and many will include the name of the purchasing manager or office manager. This is the person you will want to speak with: the Purchasing Manager or Office Manager.

How to obtain the Purchasing Manager or Office Manager's name

If your list does not give you the name of the purchasing manager, you can simply call the office and ask the receptionist, "Could you please tell me the name of your purchasing manager?" Usually, they give you his name without any problem. If the receptionist says that they don't have a purchasing manager then the next best question is, "What is the name of the person who would hire employees?" Many times this will be the same person that will look after the hiring of the cleaning company. When the receptionist gives you the name, then you simply ask, "Is he there now?" If he is in, the receptionist puts you through, usually without any questions.

Some receptionists and secretaries however, are trained to screen their manager's calls, and in doing so will determine, on their own, the manager's decision. This is usually the case in larger corporate offices or larger insurance company offices. They may ask you your name and Company Name and why you want to speak to their boss. Our reply is usually our name, the first three letters of our Company

Name and state that it's a business or private matter. We generally don't have any problems.

Only once in many years have I had great difficulty getting past the secretary or receptionist. Even at that I ended up getting the contract a little time down the road.

A Telephone Presentation

When you speak to the Purchasing Manager or Office manager try to have a pleasant relaxed tone in your voice. Be calm and cool. It is necessary that there are no distracting noises in the background while you are talking to him. Distracting noises may include loud talking from family, children screaming or crying or even a television or radio in the background. You will want to sound as professional as possible with the least amount of background noise as possible.

When you speak with the manager you simply tell him your name, your company name and that you would be happy to clean his office. Here is the phone presentation that we use.

"Good afternoon - How are you today?" Pause - wait for their reply. "That's great (usually the response is positive). My name is (insert your name here - first and last name) and I'm with "XYZ Janitorial Services (insert your company name here) and what I'm calling you about is that we are very interested in the Janitorial Cleaning of your offices. We were wondering if we could send someone down to give you a free estimate without obligation on the cleaning of your offices."

This presentation sounds very simple. But simple is good. This is the very presentation that we have used for years and years with absolute great success. Keep it simple. You are not a telemarketer - as such. Basically, the end result is that you want his permission to come down and see him and then give him a free estimate on cleaning his office.

The manager's response will be immediate. You will know where you stand right away. The answer will be yes, or no or we're happy right now, or call me back later.

IMPORTANT: It is important to make notes on all your calls regarding the information that you have gained: purchasing manager's name, and dates on which you called him, his response and any other information that would be helpful that will assist you later when you call him back. I use a lined notepad from the local office supply store and use one page per prospective client. Anytime I need to refer back to information about a particular prospective client, all his information is on one page.

If he asks you to call him back, make sure you do just that and when you do call him back tell him that "**he asked you to call back**". If he says that he is happy with his present service ask him, "Would it be ok if I called you back in a couple of months or so?" Usually, without hesitation he says "sure." Make a note of this and call him back.

NOTE: If he says that he is happy with the company he presently has cleaning his offices ask him who his present cleaners are. Most managers will tell you the name of the company. Keep this on your records, you might find it useful later. If a prospective client says that he's happy, ask for his permission to send him some literature about your services. If he gives the Okay, send him your advertising letter. It's also a good idea to call him back from time to time; perhaps at the end of each month or every other month. This way you always keep your name and services before him. If he has difficulties with his present cleaners he is more likely to give you a call.

Keep in mind that if he says he is happy with his current cleaning company, don't take this as a defeat, but rather take this as an opportunity to build a relationship with him for future business purposes. This works wonders. Continue to follow him up.

Method 4.

The use of the telephone book is also another good source. Simply go through the telephone book and call each prospective business, ask for the purchasing manager or office manager and then explain your services as noted above. I haven't found this particular method beneficial for us. However, you might find it a really good method for you in your particular location.

Method 5.

Property management firms are another good source. Many larger buildings have a property management company looking after all the cares and concerns - including the cleaning - of their building. Contact these companies, explain your services, and send them some literature. Property management companies usually handle more than one building which in turn would allow you the opportunity to bid on any of their buildings.

We had one property management company that we provided cleaning services for and actually ended up getting the contracts for each of their buildings. In fact when they built a new building they handed our contract to their new tenants along with their own lease. Each tenant still had to make a choice, but it got our foot in the door in a great way.

Method 6.

Another good way of reaching prospective clients is that of "Householder Mail". **This is perhaps one of the best ways to obtain contracts.** Using this method, together with the Direct Phone contact method mentioned above, we have built a very successful business.

Depending on which country you live in, the Post Office has divided each city or town into "walks" or "routes" that each postal carrier is responsible to service. Each walk contains a certain number of houses and businesses. You can make arrangements with the Post Office to use this "Householder Mail" delivery and even specify that they will deliver your advertising letters only to "Businesses". The cost and details of this "Householder Mail" method will vary according to the country you live in and or the state/province in which you reside. Looking into this method could prove to be an excellent way of obtaining business. We have found this method to be very, very successful.

In using this method you will prepare an advertising letter (see our sample), place it in a white business envelope - with no name or address on the envelope and then let the Post Office mail it for you at a reduced rate. The cost is usually at a fraction of the cost of sending it by regular mail. The only notation that we have put on the envelope is: Attention Purchasing Manager.

We have found that the Post Office will allow this because this is not an address and thus still classifies as "Unaddressed Mail". This addition of "Attention Purchasing Manager" is very important to you because your unaddressed letter needs to get into the right hands. Again, the actual working out of this method may vary from location to location.

12

THE APPOINTMENT

Whichever method you have used to introduce your services to a client, when he says "Yes" he'd like a free estimate on the cleaning of his offices you will need to make an appointment to tour his offices and speak with him regarding his cleaning needs. In making the appointment, never make the appointment for the same day.

When we schedule appointments we always schedule them for the next day or even the next again. This might sound silly, but it has been an important key for us.

In arranging your appointments, try to set as many on the same day as possible. Each appointment should be set an hour apart. This hour will give you time to tour his office, explain your services and provide ample traveling time between appointments with even the odd coffee break thrown in.

In touring his office make sure you have a pen and pad to make notes regarding number of desks, number of private offices, the general office congestion, washrooms, and any particular cleaning requests he may have.

In many cases the manager will give you a tour very briskly. Don't let this bother you. This is one of the reasons why you need some notes. I have learned to walk quickly through an office and remember the layout for weeks. Having said this, keep in mind that the manager is familiar with the office, but you are not. So take notes - most Janitorial Companies do. MORE ON THIS LATER.

13

MARKETING STRATEGIES THAT WORK - PART 2

HOW TO GET CONTRACTS AND LEADS

Besides the methods I have explained in the previous chapter, I wanted to add a few additional ways that you could obtain contracts and leads for your business.

With a tremendous increase in the past years of the effectiveness and benefits of Social Media, this gives us a business people other opportunities to let people know about our business services. Someone has said that if a business is not on Social Media, then they are not worth doing business with. That seems like a harsh saying, but in today's fast paced world that seems to be a reality.

Here are a few examples of Social Media for you to consider.

FaceBook:

Facebook is one of the fastest growing Social Media platforms currently on the internet. If you do not already have a FaceBook account you can sign up for one. It is free to do so. Once you are signed up with your own page you can add a business page that can then be used for your cleaning business. This is very easy to do and only takes a few minutes.

Having a Facebook presence will give you a sense of stability and professionalism in the eyes of your prospective clients. You can place your FaceBook (business page) on your website, business cards and advertising media. To call attention to your FaceBook address you could put a nice look arrow or saying that says, "Find Us On FaceBook", then place your address beside or below that title.

Although setting up a business FaceBook page is not difficult, you might not know where to begin or how to actually go about doing this. There are lots of very helpful YouTube videos that will take through the various steps on how to do this. Here is a search listing for setting up a business FaceBook page. https://goo.gl/DnmPm1

When you go to that link you will notice that the two top videos listed are advertising, but the ones below are free. Free is nice!

For your FaceBook business fan page you will also need to have what is called a "banner or Cover." This is a image that will reflect what you or your business is about. The banner/cover is what a person will see when they first come to your FaceBook page.

This banner is also not difficult to create and install. Again, YouTube can come to the rescue to show you how to do this. In addition, if you are not creative with graphics programs you can get your banner created for you for $5 at fiver. Fiver is a platform where many people offer their services for only $5.

Here are the links for you to consider in terms of YouTube tutorials for banners. The second link is for fiver so you can consider having someone create the banner for you. Just type these links into your favorite browser.

https://goo.gl/ppU4W9 Youtube

https://goo.gl/ohi2yB Fiverr

Your Own Business Website

Another great way to help obtain contracts and leads is to have your own business website. This might sound scary at first if you are not familiar with websites, but it is a great way to get your brand out there and let people know all about your business.

The cost is actually very small. This is contrary to many people who feel that a professional business website can cost thousands of dollars. Quite to the contrary it doesn't need to. You can have an awesome professional website for "almost" nothing. Ah ... you might say, how much is the "almost?" If you proceed the way I am suggesting the approximate cost will be $15 per year for a domain name and $10 per month for hosting. That is it. Really, that is very economical.

Now, many people do not know where to start or how to go about building their own business website. Well, YouTube comes to the rescue again with some really great tutorials. I would like to recommend a particular tutorial to you that will guide you through everything that needs to be done - step by step and very easy.

If you follow the tutorial you will have your website up and running in less than one day. Here is the tutorial that will allow you to make an "awesome" website for your business. See it here https://goo.gl/12KxrL. I know you will be impresses with both this tutorials and the website that you will build. Have a look and let me know what you think.

YouTube Video Platform

YouTube is another consideration for your business. YouTube is growing so fast that it is hard to keep up with the statistics. Millions of people are watching YouTube videos every day. Prospective client's could be watching the videos about your business and calling you asking for a pricing on your services.

In order to begin on YouTube you will need to sign up for a free account. If you already have a Google Mail account you can just sign into YouTube using your Google Mail account sign in credentials.

Placing your business videos on YouTube is as easy as uploading them to your YouTube account. Making the videos can be very easy also. There are three ways you can do this on the cheap.

1. Have someone at fiverr make a promo video for you for $5.
2. If you have a SmartPhone with a camera that can take videos - make a video of yourself sitting behind a desk or standing against a wall explaining your services.
3. Use PowerPoint and a Screen Recording software and a microphone head set and explain your services with you as a voice over.

For the first option here is a link of people at fiver that can make a video for you for $5. https://goo.gl/bsSySW

For the second option of using a SmartPhone, here is a search list for "How To Do's" See here

For the third option of using PowerPoint, here, again is a search list of "How To Do" https://goo.gl/iH5iqA

For the Screen Recording software you can use the free Screencast O Matic - http://screencast-o-matic.com/

You could also use Camtasia for Windows Screen Recording Software or if you have a Mac, you could use ScreenFlow. The only drawback from these two products is that they cost money. Personally, I have used the free and paid ($15/yr) version of Screencast O Matic and really liked it. Currently I use ScreenFlow on my Mac because it will do much more than the others.

Whichever way you decide to make your video, you would upload it to YouTube and then place a link for that video on your website so your visitors could watch it and enjoy it. Great free advertising and a great help to build your brand.

Craig's List And Kajiji

Both of these online platforms are what is called free online classified advertising. You may be familiar with Craig's List already. Kanji is the Canadian version, which is owned by Ebay. Craig's List is also available through Canada as well. Check where you are living and see if these are available to you and if not what compatible online classified advertising would be available.

Both of these online classified advertising platforms allow you to place free advertising about your cleaning business throughout the area that you desire to service. You would just pick the state/province and city/town you desire and go from there. You can, of course, upgrade and pay for more bells and whistles in terms of advertising, but so many businesses just use the regular free classified advertising. Again, free is great.

FaceBook Ads

I have left this part till now because I didn't want any confusion with FaceBook Pages with FaceBook Ads. If you have been on FaceBook you will notice that there will appear "Sponsored Story" type of advertisements in your timeline. You will also notice there are ads located on the right side of your FaceBook page. The advertisements that are directly on your timeline are the best ones to consider.

These timeline advertisements, if you were to click anthem would take you to an offer or a business website. You can also advertise using FaceBook advertisements the same way.

Using FaceBook advertising will allow you to be very specific in terms of the clients you want to see your ad and their geographical location.

However, a caution using FaceBook ads is needed here. If you decide to go this route be very careful that you limit your daily spending to a very comfortable amount or you could have a run-a-way account that you might have difficulty paying. Be very cautious.

If you are interested in looking into FaceBook advertising here is a search link that will give you some details: See here . Again, ignore the videos that are marked "advertisements" and enjoy watching the free video tutorials.

14

HIRING WORKERS

Depending on what size you desire your cleaning business to grow to, you might find yourself in need of help. This is where you would consider hiring workers for your cleaning business.

If you goals for your cleaning business is to only obtain enough cleaning contracts to bring in a small part time income to help pay for some extra bills or save up for a special item, then, you might be happy to just clean the offices yourself and save the castle of hiring workers.

Many a couple obtain 3-5 cleaning contracts, clean them themselves and are very happy to keep it that way. They can plan when they will do the cleaning and then plan their activities and weekends around their money making cleaning business. And there is nothing wrong with that at all. The great thing about the cleaning business is that you can make it as big or small as you desire.

You can really customize the cleaning business to your own lifestyle and desires. This way you can have a nice income producing business that you can scale up if you desire, but keep it as a casual part time business on the side.

On the other hand if your approach to the cleaning business is not that of a casual approach and you want to scale it up to whatever you would like to have, then there will come a time when you will need to hire workers to help you.

In our own cleaning business we always had people working for us. We found it much easier and faster to have many hands doing the work rather than just one person. We operated, most of the time, in what is called a "Crew System." This means that we had at least 2 people up to 5 or more people going into each office together to provide cleaning services.

Using the Crew System of say 5 people, each person would have a specific last to do in the cleaning process. I have explained this in detail in this book, so I won't repeat myself here.

By the way - you can run your cleaning business using the Crew System, scale it up and still only need to work part time in the business while bringing in some serious income. This is what we did and enjoyed the benefits.

Now back to the topic of hiring workers. When the tie comes to hire workers you will want them to be "experienced" in office cleaning. You will also want them to be bondable and provide you with references. It is also very wise for you to call these references and make sure they are legitimate and are not a relative of some sort of the person who wants to work for you.

When we needed to hire workers we just ran a small advertisement in the classified section of our local newspaper. It would go something like this:

Office Cleaner wanted by local Janitorial company to work evening hours. Must be experienced, dependable and bondable. Serious enquiries only. (243)542-7896.

We would then have someone answer the phone when people called. This person would ask specific questions and run the answers on a lined piece of paper. Here are some of the questions that might be asked:

- Are you experience in Commercial Office Cleaning?
- How long have you been doing Office Cleaning?
- What were you duties in your Office Cleaning job(s)?
- Do you have a SS Card? You won't ask for the number now - but the answer will indicate if they qualify to work in your state/province.
- Do you still work for a cleaning company? You don't want your competition sending spies
- If not - why are you no longer working for the previous cleaning company?
- What other cleaning companies have you worked for and for how long?
- What is the name of your previous cleaning company employer?
- What hours in the evening would you be available?
- How many hours work are you looking for?
- Can you provide three (3) references that are NOT related to you in any way?
- When references given - What relationship do you have with this person(s)?
- Do you have a high school diploma, college degree?
- Do you have a resume you could send me?

The above questions are all good questions that you would need to know the answers to before hiring workers. After all you will be trusting them in the premises of your client's and your reputation will be on the line.

You could also have these possible workers fill out an application form that would contain the questions above. You could have them fill out the form in person or fill out the form online on your website. However, we have found dealing with them on the telephone, as mentioned above, will give you faster and better results.

Hiring workers is not scary or something to be avoided if you need help. However, caution and thorough checking out of the individual is always a wise thing to do.

Deductions:

It would be advisable for you to check with your local state/province and also your federal governments and find out what deductions will be required to be deducted from your worker's paycheck. Each level of government will have their helpful literature that will give you all the information you will need.

When you hire workers it is very important that you keep accurate records of hours worked, pay rate that you are paying them, their gross paycheck and their net paycheck indicating the amount of every deduction and the time period it covers.

In addition you will need to know the amounts that you will need to pay the various governments as an employer.

We have found it much easier to have our bookkeeper take care of all our payroll needs. Our bookkeeper calculated the correct deductions, made out the checks, reported amounts to the various governments, told us how much we needed to pay as an employer and much more. Again, as I have mentioned in another chapter, the cost for the services of a good bookkeeper is more than worth the money.

By hiring a bookkeeper we were able to concentrate on the business of growing our business rather than getting side tracked by items that could be taken care of by a bookkeeper.

Getting a bookkeeper or not will, of course, be something that you will need to decide for yourself.

15

HOW TO PRICE OFFICES FOR PROFIT

There are basically three ways to price an office. **The Utilization of all three methods for any pricing opportunity is recommended.**

One thing to keep in mind when pricing is that you are not working for them as a cleaning lady on an hourly basis in which your pay can vary from week to week, but rather you are a business person, running a Professional Business.

Therefore, because of this, you will be pricing their required cleaning on a "contract basis", in which you will contract to do certain cleaning functions for an agreed upon price. Additional services beyond the normal cleaning duties will be invoiced as additional charges. This is clearly understood by most business people.

NOTE: In your pricing keep in mind that whatever holidays your client gets so do you - with pay. You don't adjust your price just because they are closed for three days at Christmas. If you come across a client that wants you to deduct holidays from your price - it would be better not to have him as a client.

Now.... let's look at various methods of pricing.

First Method.

The first method is called the "Square Foot Method". This is a very simple method and is simply used to obtain an approximate, sometimes accurate, price for an office. To use this method you must determine the square footage of the office. This can be done by asking the manager the square footage. Some managers will know the square footage of their building or offices. If he doesn't know the square footage don't press him, there are other ways to determine this.

If he doesn't know the square footage and if his office has a suspended ceiling (dropped ceiling) you could also simply count the ceiling tiles - which are usually 2'X4' and then multiplying the calculated square footage by the current rate. Some suspended ceilings have fancier tiles which are 2'X2'; if so, just count accordingly.

Depending on where you are located, the current rate will vary from place to place. In some areas the current rate is about 15-25 cents per/sq. ft. This will give a price per month for a basic, no frills five nights a week service. If the desired service is less than five nights a week then the price can be recalculated to suit. If the service is to be less than five nights a week, then the cost per cleaning will be more because it will generally need more cleaning.

NOTE: As already mentioned above, the method using the per square foot rates will vary according to your location and country. To determine the current rate is not difficult and can be accomplished by using the other methods described further in this book.

In using the square foot method - If the office has 70 ceiling tiles 2' across and 60 ceiling tiles 4' long then the size of the office would be 33,600 sq. ft. and an approximate price would be 33,600 X 15 cents = $5040.00 per month for a "basic" five night a week service.

NOTE: This price is based on a standard cleaning with no extras. By extras we mean plant watering, *window cleaning (unless you decide to have them included in the price), washing dishes, carpet shampooing, etc. We have found this method successful in pricing offices of 4000 sq. ft. or more.

*Regarding window cleaning - in any given estimate the office front doors are always included in the estimate of cleaning. The exception would be if the office has multiple entrances with many glass entrance doors.

Limitations:

This method is not always accurate when used to price smaller offices of around 1-2,000 sq. ft., and thus all three pricing methods should be used to obtain the finished price. As a rule of thumb - use this method to calculate an approximate price and confirm the amount using the other two methods.

As noted in this section - the general congestion of an office needs to be taken into consideration. If the office is congested, this method would need to be subsidized by the other methods to obtain a more accurate estimate.

Second Method:

The second method is called the "Comparison Method". Simply by comparing the prospective office with another office that you are presently cleaning or have cleaned in the past will assist you in coming up with a fair price. Thus comparing the frequency of the cleaning (number of times per week); the number of side offices and any particular details you have with a contract you are familiar with.

One advantage of this method is that if you are presently cleaning an office and if you feel it is priced slightly under what you should be getting you can make the correct adjustment with the new office. This method is perhaps the best and easiest because you can use what you have in terms of client's offices and then use that to price the offices you want.

Third Method:

This method is called the "Detailed Method". Here you will, after having toured the prospective office and having made some notes, estimate the time required for each job (vacuuming, dusting, garbage, etc.) on a nightly basis. By adding and multiplying, a total price per month can be established. Your estimated time for each job should be based on how long it would take an "experienced" cleaner to perform the required task. This method is also good for offices that are congested with a lot of desks and tight spaces to vacuum. It is also a good method to use if the office you are estimating doesn't have good quality carpet or very old floors, etc.

FOR EXAMPLE: To clean XYZ Company would take:

10 minutes to empty the garbage

15 minutes to vacuum the carpets

15 minutes to dust the desks etc.

8 minutes to clean the washrooms

5 minutes to clean the front door both sides (if only one)

Total time and price: (An example)

53 minutes per night

X 5 nights per week = 265 minutes per week

X 4.23 weeks per month = 1120.95 minutes per month

divided by 60 = (18.68) 19 hours/month

X how much you want to make per hour (* or current rate)

= a monthly price.

+ the cost of travel (if applicable) equipment & supplies - usually 10 - 20%

= a total monthly price.

NOTE: The * current rate varies from place to place. If you were working for yourself and do not intend to hire people - then you can have an advantage by charging a little less. However, if you intend to hire people and pay them wages - then you must consider increasing your current rate. The current rate will include what you want to make as a profit plus any employment costs you may encounter such as Worker's Compensation, pension costs, etc.

When, and if the time comes to hire people to do the work for you it would be a good idea to check with your Tax offices and Labor offices to make sure that you know what is to be deducted from their pay (income tax, unemployment, etc.) and what you need to pay as well. Once these details are known you simply put them into your calculations.

When we first started out in the cleaning we found it better to do the work ourselves rather than hiring people to help until it was absolutely necessary. This gives you a competitive edge over some of your competition and it could be reflected in the pricing you give to your clients as well.

As our business grew we began to hire people and ended up with crews of people. Whether you hire people to help or just do it yourself will be according to what your plans and desires are for your own business. It is totally up to you as to how big or how small you want your business to be.

The pricing guidelines in this section are the pricing guidelines that we follow. However, you may find it necessary to make adjustments wherever you see fit. We have found these guidelines to be successful and the completed price arrived at, using these methods of pricing, is very competitive with our competition.

However, keep in mind that an office that would take 30 minutes per night to clean - that same office size could take 60 minutes if it were very congested. Congestion is a key factor. Some offices are cramped and really need a bigger office space to do their business, but at the present they are making do with the smaller space they have.

Remember, if you tour an office that is very congested with lots of desks and cabinets that are close together and an abnormal number of electrical cords or cables stretched over the floor - you need to know that if it is not a carpeted floor, it will take you longer to sweep that floor because you will need to pick up or move each cord.

However; if it is a carpeted area, it is much easier to vacuum because you don't always have to pick up the cords. Many times you can simply move them aside with the vacuum cleaner. It all depends on how the congestion is presented. But in any event, keep the congestion factor in mind. You need to ask yourself, "How long would it take you to clean in that type of environment?"

16

THE DETAILED METHOD FURTHER EXPLAINED

Time & Pricing

In pricing an office and estimating the time required, allow 2-3 minutes to dust each desk. This will include the desk top, and any other horizontal surfaces close by, computer and screen and the telephone. If the computer is turned on do not dust the computer keyboard. You could inadvertently press a key and do all kinds of interesting things.

When cleaning telephones you need to remove the hand set from the telephone and wipe the mouth piece and ear piece area. Also clean the areas that the handset fits into on the cradle. Some cleaning company's staff carry in their back pocket a separate duster slightly damp with a cleaner disinfectant that they use to wipe the ear and mouth piece of the phone and the cradle in which they sit. Using a disinfectant for this can also be a great selling point when explaining your services to potential clients. This is especially true during the cold and flu season.

IMPORTANT: Time and time again we have had prospective clients tell us that their present cleaners don't clean their phones properly -

if at all. I have actually seen people get angry over this and that's why they called us to give them a price. In more cases than not, we have obtained business because of the sloppiness of some cleaning companies. Cleaning the phones is an important item not to miss.

We allow about 3-4 minutes for dusting the president's office which will contain more items to dust - such as a credenza, additional coffee tables, etc.

With regards to vacuuming, we generally allow 2 minutes to vacuum a small private office and 3-5 minutes to vacuum a Board Room or executive office (more time because of the increased number of chairs and or furniture).

We allow 1 minute per garbage bin to empty and approximately 5 minutes to clean a washroom (a general cleaning only). This includes cleaning the fixtures, mirror, and replenishing the paper supply. You can add in additional time for a more thorough cleaning, usually done on the weekend from time to time.

NOTE: The 5 minute cleaning time mentioned above is a washroom with one toilet, one sink, and one mirror. Multiple fixture washrooms will take more time in direct relation to the number of fixtures - so make the proper allowances in your time estimations. Also, remember that these time estimations will be for an experienced cleaner and not someone who will take 60 minutes to clean a set of sink taps.

We allow 5 minutes to clean the front glass entrance door (if the door is completely glass); less if only partially glass, but usually not less than 3 minutes.

The above estimations are for a 5 night a week service and are based on one person who is familiar with cleaning. That is, a regular nightly cleaning that consistently keeps the cleaning up to par so that a lot of time is not required to maintain it.

However, in working on an estimated cost for a once a week or twice a week service, you will need to take into consideration that it must be worth your while to drive to the office, unload the cleaning equipment, do the cleaning and come home again. In addition, a once a week service or twice a week service is not kept up on a regular nightly basis - so it will have more accumulation of dirt on the floors, carpets, washrooms and front entrances, etc. Therefore there will be more cleaning required in terms of time and supplies than that of a regular 5 night a week service.

The dirtier the office the more you will charge in time and supplies. For example: a trucking company or cement company will need more time and supplies to clean than a lawyer's office. So keep this in mind when you price.

Someone might ask in terms of cleaning frequency per week "well would it not work out to be the same in the end anyway?" Our experience has been that it doesn't. We have gone into trucking companies weekly or bi-weekly and spent far more time and supplies that we would have if we did it nightly. And even at that, **the type of office/industry you are cleaning will make a great difference to your time, supplies and profit.**

Our personal preference has been to stay away from any contract that was not 5 nights a week. We have found that the more routine type of cleaning contracts we were able to obtain, the more we could efficiently schedule the nightly cleaning. This of course reflected on greater profits.

However, you may choose to go beyond simply staying with 5 night a week contracts. And that is great. Don't forget you are the boss of your own business. We have found that even the type of industry our client was involved in makes a difference to us. See below for more details.

The Type of Offices You Clean Does Matter.

17

HOW TO SUBMIT YOUR QUOTATION

In this section we will be dealing mainly with presenting your services to a prospective client in person. This will deal with submitting a quotation in writing using what we call a "Service Outline". We will discuss the various elements of the actual Service Outline a little further on in this book. But for now, we will deal with submitting a quotation and the various elements involved with this.

Submitting quotations in the proper manner is important. We usually give our clients a quotation in a Special Presentation folder or a plastic spine bound folder with their company name, address, city and province/state on the front and our name on the bottom. This is similar to a "Title Page". See the sample service outline cover.

The important point to remember is that your presentation will speak in ways that you could not. A neat, business like, professional looking presentation should reflect on your professionalism and draw their attention to your company. You will find this Presentation to be a very valuable business tool for you.

Once you have arrived at a total monthly cost for the cleaning of your client's office, the next step would be to call him and tell him what the price is and ask him what he thinks of it. We have done this over and over again with great success. Usually, the response will be immediate. If he feels it's too high he'll tell you it is too high. We have asked our prospective clients "how much too high is it?" They have told us plainly. We have then had the opportunity to examine our pricing to see if it would be feasible to adjust it.

In our experience, once we arrived at the finished price and told our client what the price was on the telephone, we then told him that we would draw up a "Service Outline" for him and then ask if we could stop by and see him for a few minutes to give him the "Service Outline". The client usually said "OK" and then we set the day (usually the next day) and the time.

Some clients however, will ask you to just drop it off in the office to their attention - if this is what they request - then go for it. In this case remember to call him back within two days and ask if he received it, has he had an opportunity to look at it, and what he thinks of it.

If he hasn't had an opportunity to look at it just ask him if you could call him back in a few days. Usually that's not a problem. We have found that most of the time you will be able to present your "Service Outline" in person to your client. Don't forget that follow up is very important.

In the actual presentation of your "service outline" make sure you give your client the original copy to read over in full, while both of you are together. Also make sure that you have a photocopy of the same outline for yourself, not only for your own records but in case, during the presentation of your "Service Outline", he asks you any questions. This way you can quickly refer to the area or page that he is asking about or referring to.

When you are in your client's office, sit in a relaxed position, confident that you know what you are talking about. Don't fidget, bite your fingernails or look around his office. During your presentation of your Service Outline you may wish to point out specific parts of the

Service Outline that would be of particular interest to your client. This could include areas that he has perhaps mentioned to you on your initial tour of his office. Perhaps there may be something the other cleaners are not doing, or perhaps do not include in their present cleaning. If you have or will include these missed items in your price make mention of this not only on your original tour of his office but **AGAIN POINT OUT** these benefits to him at this time.

Remember never speak badly of any other cleaning company - even if your client does. Just make sure that you assure him that "your cleaning company" will be more than pleased to take care of all his needs... and make sure you do.

Before the presentation, we have found it a great idea to think of any questions he may ask during the presentation and have an answer ready. Be relaxed, confident and sure of yourself. You are a business person and you have a much needed service to offer. In general, don't be too talkative while your client is reading the outline. Depending on whether or not he asks any questions, you may want to leave pointing out parts of the outline until after he has read it.

NOTE: As mentioned above, before you spend the time to prepare a Service Outline telephone the client and mention that you have calculated a price for him. Tell him your price and ask him what he thinks. If your price is too high, chances are he will tell you, thus giving you time to make up a finished presentation with a little reduction in the price - if possible. If your price is too high you can ask him how much higher it is. He probably won't tell you exactly but will give you a general idea.

FOLLOW UP - General Review

Follow up is another important key to securing clients and also provides an opportunity to deal with any questions regarding your cleaning Service Outline.

After you have given your client the formal written "Service Outline" (quotation) you can give him a call two days later, and ask him if he has any questions regarding the outline. Also ask him what he thinks of the outline in general and note his comments. He may have some questions which can be easily answered over the phone.

You might also want to ask him when he would consider changing to your service. Play it by ear, this is basically what we do and find it effective. If the client wants time to further read the outline and consult his superiors, ask when you should call him back and make a note of his answer.

Don't forget to call back, and tell him when you do call back that he suggested you call at this time.

18

HOW TO KEEP YOUR CONTRACTS

An important key to remember in the cleaning business is that your customer is always right and that you are providing a valuable service. Sometimes your client may ask you to do something extra. Perhaps wash some dishes, or a window or whatever.

You will find that if you do a few little extras when asked, without charging him for it - these favors will pay off in the long run. That is without charging, if the time required is not excessive.

If you are asked to do a sink of dishes on a nightly basis, then you may wish to consider charging an additional fee for this service. In all the years that we have done cleaning only once did we do a set of dishes for a client. It was a onetime thing and we never made a habit of doing it. No other clients have asked us to do dishes.

We would have done the occasional dish if requested - only if it didn't largely upset the cleaning routine of that office and the general scheduling of other offices being cleaned that night. You will need to ultimately use your own judgment.

19

ABOUT YOUR TELEPHONE

Always make sure that your telephone is answered in a businesslike manner. It is not a good idea to have children answer your telephone. You are running a business and business people expect a business answer to their call. It is very important to your clients that they feel you are available to talk to and answer their needs at any time.

Although you don't want to be in bondage to your phone you may consider an automatic telephone answering machine, or even an answering service. We have found that the easiest way to take care of phone calls is to have our home office phone "call forwarded" to our cell phone. This way we can go about doing our business or have personal time or whatever and yet still be available if clients or new business come calling.

Cell phones can allow you to have a virtual office in your pocket and allow you to not be hampered at all in what you want to do or where you want to go. Most cell phones have call display. Should a client call you and you are unable to take the call at that moment they can leave a message on your phone. You will have their message, their telephone number and the time they called. If your client leaves a message asking you to get back to them - get back to them as soon as possible. This is only good service and will pay big rewards later.

I have actually had clients who did leave a message on my phone (I wasn't able to take the call at the time) and I called them back quickly - they commented on how much they appreciated how quickly I got back to them. Good business.

I remember one client who noticed that I had my cell phone in my pocket commenting that he was so glad that I was available at any time. He went on to say that he was so tired of leaving messages on other answering machines and waiting for a full day or more before they even got back to him. Remember it is not wrong to have the client leave a message on your phone, but it is important to get back to him quickly.

In the years that we have been in the cleaning business rarely have we received complaints or even lost contracts. Actually, there have been times that we terminated a contract. This Termination or cancellation feature is built into the "Service Outline". I will explain this feature a little further along in this book. However, if your client does call you with a complaint, the way in which you handle the complaint can pay dividends later. Remember 99% of the time, the client is right.

If you have a client that has a complaint, ensure him that you understand the problem and that you will personally take care of the matter. Arguing of course is out of the question. We must not be argumentative. Always try to be helpful in a pleasant way.

If the complaint is the result of a service that you are not providing at the time, but yet they expect it to be included - simply explain to them that you would be pleased to provide that service but there would be an additional charge since this was not included in the original Service Outline. However, if the additional service that is being requested is very minor, you may want to include it without any additional cost. This also pays big dividends later.

The cleaning business has enough profit in it that you can do some "small" things without charging, still make a profit and keep your clients happy beyond the Service Outline. Even if you expand in the cleaning business and have people working for you or even a crew of people (we did) you can still do some "small" things and it won't cost you anything, but will reward you with good favor in your client's eyes.

NOTE: What do we mean when we say that it "pays big dividends later"? In our contacting potential clients we have found that periodically even though they were not totally happy with their cleaners they wanted to continue with them because their present cleaners were doing one or two little extras without charging for them.

These little extras that their present cleaning company was doing did not cost the cleaning company a penny but did result in client loyalty for a time. It is important to understand that doing little extras for nothing is not a reason for doing a poor job. Eventually, a poor job will catch up with you and another company will get the contract.

Therefore it is important to go over the "Service Outline" with your client at the beginning of your cleaning relationship with him in order to avoid any misunderstandings. This will ensure that everything your client requests will be in your "Service Outline".

In the cleaning business, as long as you do a good job, and this is really not hard at all, you should have no complaints or problems. You will just continue to clean their offices year after year and bank their check month after month. We have had cleaning contracts for years.

20

HOW AND WHEN TO INVOICE
YOUR CLIENTS FOR BEST RESULTS

Invoicing your accounts is very simple. You do not need fancy or expensive stationery invoices unless you really want to go that route. We have simply used our letterhead. On it we have typed the date, our client's name and address below the date and the words:

"Cleaning for the month of .... (Insert amount)"

This statement would be on the left side of the page and the monthly amount would be on the right side of the page. This is all we have done and it is very satisfactory. Please see the sample invoice as an example.

When to Send Out Your Invoice

We send our invoices out on the 25th of each month, and bill them for the full month. For example, if cleaning for January is $500.00. You would send your client an invoice on January 25th for $500.00. We also print on the invoice the words "Net 10 days." This means that we are asking the client to pay the bill within 10 days of receipt of the invoice.

Most clients will do this without any problems. This helps you to obtain your income quickly instead of just leaving it open ended and wondering when they will get around to paying you. In all the years that we have been in the Cleaning Business there has only been a couple of clients who were slow in paying and only one that I can think of that we terminated the contract because they didn't want to pay their bills.

We have found that if a client is overly slow in paying or if we have to continually call them to find out when they are going to pay us - that client isn't worth having. Fortunately, we haven't had those kinds of clients, with the exceptions mentioned above. You don't generally have any problems with payment when you stick with commercial contracts.

Invoicing of clients five days before the end of the month allows the client time to process the invoice in a speedy manner. However; having said that, there may be clients who will need a little more time to process the payment because of company policies, check signing practices and such. Even with this we found that we still received our payments in a quick manner.

21

HOW TO CLEAN YOUR OFFICES

In this chapter we will look at how to clean your client's office and what is involved in the cleaning. There will be some YouTube links to help illustrate the point being made.

Dusting

Part of your cleaning practices will involve dusting of desks, countertops, and many other horizontal surfaces. These will be somewhat similar to your own home, except that now it will involve dusting office furniture instead. Dusting is pretty well straight forward. The most important tools that you will use will be cotton dusting cloths and a "Swiffer type" duster.

You probably know what a Swiffer duster is - it is the duster that is like a feather duster on a handle and is treated with a dust magnet chemical. They are inexpensive and do a wonderful job. They can be readily obtained from the local supermarket or some Janitorial Supply Houses.

Most of the desks in the modern offices are of the pre-finished top type – in other words they are not real wood. Because of this you can simply use a damp cloth to clean most of the desks and use a Swiffer type duster to get into hard to reach parts or areas that are more congested.

The only desks that you can't use a damp cloth on are desks made with real wood. For these you use a dry cloth with furniture polish applied as required. You don't need a lot of furniture polish and it is easily obtained through a Janitorial Supply House or even, depending on how many cans you want, cheaper at the local supermarket. Pledge Furniture Polish is our favorite and we have used it for years.

With regards to cloth dusters, we use rental dusting cloths that do not leave any lint, but you may choose not to use rental cloths. Whatever you decide, make sure that the duster is not made of material that will leave lint or pieces of the fabric behind through use and that the duster is large enough to fold in four. Simply rinse the cloth under the tap and wring it out until it is only damp - not wet, but damp, and use the cloth in the same manner as you would wipe your kitchen table.

Remember, this is for non-wood desks and furniture. We have found that using a damp cloth on a real wood desk or furniture will tend to discolor and stain the furniture. This is why we use a dry cloth and furniture polish on real wood products.

The reason for having the cloth folded in four is so that you can turn the cloth to the clean side after the side you're using gets dirty. By doing this it will give you eight sides to use. We have chosen to use damp cloths to dust with in preference to other methods because damp cloths will remove finger marks, coffee rings and general soil in one operation without the need of repeated cleaning and, in most cases, without the use of cleaning liquids.

We don't spray cleaners on desk or use cleaning liquids in the cloth itself. We have found that if we use cleaning liquids it tends to leave a film on the desk. Your customers will complain.

Usually one cloth will clean an entire office with two or three rinses: depending on the size and cleanliness of the office. The more desks in the office and/or the dirtier the office is, the greater the number of times you'll have to rinse the cloth. This same duster can be used to dust the desks, phones, and other items which require dusting. We have found that it is generally inexpensive to always have a generous supply of clean dusters with us at all times.

If a duster gets too dirty we just put the dirty duster in a pail or bag and grab another duster- damp it and away we go. This is an excellent way of getting the job done right and getting it done quickly.

We have found that Swiffer type dusters are great for dusting computer monitors and keyboards. Make sure that the computer is not turned on when you dust the keyboard. If it is on it would be best to leave the keyboard for another time. Make sure that the monitor is turned off before dusting it. If it is on we have found it best to leave it for another time.

Again, Swiffer type dusters are great and fast for this kind of dusting because they are treated with a dust type magnet and easily remove dust without placing a lot of pressure on the duster and what is being dusted.

On a nightly cleaning job you will be basically dusting only the horizontal areas such as desks, counters, tables, etc. Window ledges are usually done once a week, or as required, as also the vertical services. We generally plan to do this additional cleaning on the weekend or at the end of the cleaning week.

Once again, a Swiffer type duster, or hand held dust mop (banister duster) will be of great help in dusting ledges, and desk sides as required. The Swiffer type duster will also help dust a desk that is too cluttered to dust in any other way.

NOTE: By the way - we have found it best to not move, sort, or compile papers on a desk, whether the desk is congested or not. We leave them exactly where they are. People get upset when their papers are moved. The "Service Outline" makes provisions for asking the client to keep his/her desk as clear of papers as possible - for dusting purposes. However, if you only need to lift a corner of a paper to remove a coffee stain or the like, go ahead.

When you dust an office don't go overboard. Basically dust what you see. In other words we don't remove typewriter or calculator covers and dust them, nor do we open filing cabinets or drawers to dust them. As a point of interest, a little off the point here, but still important, we also do not empty pencil sharpeners or three hole punch machines.

Getting Into A System/Routine:

When you go into your client's office to do the cleaning, as already mentioned above, it is important that you know where to start and develop a system or a method of doing the various cleaning operations that will get the job done well and yet will get you in and out quickly. A good system will prevent you from having to do the same job or part of it over again.

In regards to dusting, get into a system with the dusting. Start dusting in the same place every night and do the same desks - in order - each night. Doing this will increase your speed and efficiency. When you are dusting computers and monitors, don't forget to check the sides of the monitors for dust and again, as mentioned above, be careful that the computer is not turned on when you draw your hand held duster over the computer keyboard. If the computer is turned on do not turn it off. It's better to leave the keyboard until another night.

Washrooms:

Washrooms are straightforward. You simply clean the sink with a cleanser - usually very little; and clean the mirror with a damp paper towel - spray some glass cleaner on the paper towel if the mirror is in need of more than a damp paper towel. Do not use the same sponge that you cleaned the sink with. Doing this will leave white streaks on the mirror when it dries.

Clean and polish the sink faucets with a dry paper towel or if it needs more - spray a little glass cleaner on the paper towel and wipe the faucets with it. Glass cleaner is a wonderful "tool" to use for so many cleaning jobs. Clean the toilet including both sides of the toilet seat.

Make absolutely sure that the toilet bowl is clean inside. If needed, shake some cleanser in the toilet bowl and use your toilet brush to clean the bowl. If there are persistent stains then just use a toilet bowl cleaner - as you would at home.

If the washrooms include a men's urinal, make sure that the urinal is flushed well and clean the inside of the urinal with a toilet brush. You don't need to touch any of this with your hands. Many Cleaning Companies use latex gloves purchased very cheaply for the washroom cleanings. This is all very simple to do and doesn't take a lot of time to accomplish.

Some clients use deodorant blocks in the urinals to keep a fresh scent in the men's room. These are generally supplied by your client, as is the other general washroom supplies: hand towels, toilet paper, hand soap, etc. You just place a urinal block in the urinal after cleaning it and you're done - quick and simple.

Use a damp deck mop on washroom floors to pick up any drips or spills. On the weekend you will need to mop the floor more thoroughly.

Don't underestimate the importance of making sure that there are plenty of supplies in the washrooms, such as; toilet paper, hand towels, hand soap, etc. Always put an extra toilet roll on the back of the toilet and if possible place an extra package or roll of hand towels either on top of the towel dispenser or on top of the countertop.

Make sure that these additional supplies on the counter will not interfere with the general use of the sink and counter area. Making available additional washroom supplies is vitally important, especially for the ladies room. Usually the rule of thumb is that if the ladies are happy, everything goes well. It is very annoying to your client if he/she runs out of supplies at a crucial moment.

Garbage:

When emptying the garbage we find it a great asset to use a small barrel or garbage bin with wheels in which a 26X36 plastic garbage bag will fit. This barrel can be moved from desk to desk and from office to office very easily. You may wish to use a larger size bag (30X50) depending on the amount of office garbage in your client's office. Using a barrel makes the job easier, less frustrating and gets it done faster.

When you are emptying the waste paper bins, be particular about putting them back in the same place that you found them; usually under the desks or beside them. Some of the office staff are very fussy about this.

Again the key in doing the garbage in an office and actually every individual part of the cleaning is to get into a system. Start in the same place and empty the garbage in the same order each night. You will find that your speed and efficiency will increase. Also carry a very slightly damp cloth to wipe clean the ashtrays after you empty them into the garbage barrel.

It is, needless to say, that you don't use this cloth for anything else but the ashtrays. Whoever empties the garbage empties and wipes the ashtrays at the same time.

We have found that most offices have their private offices located on the outside walls or perimeter of their general office area and the general or secretarial area is usually in the center. Because of this, the system we use is a circular method.

We do the private offices in a circular method and the center office area last. Keeping this system avoids any missed rooms or missed garbage bins. As mentioned above, it is very important that the garbage bins get put back in the place and position they were in before they were emptied. People in the offices don't like changes. They also get annoyed if their office or garbage bin is missed.

NOTE: Another important point to insert here is that we generally do the garbage and dusting completely separate from other cleaning. In other words, we do not dust an office and empty the garbage at the same time. I will discuss this in further detail a little further on.

Many times we have obtained business because the cleaning service before us had attempted to do the garbage, ash trays and dusting at the same time. As a result of this, they left dust and ash on the desks because they invariably used the ash tray cloth to dust the desks and phones. As stated above, it's okay to empty the garbage, empty and wipe the ashtrays at the same time, but it is not good to include the dusting in the same operation. More on this later.

Below is the system that we have used for years and we have found that it works great. You can adapt this system to your own situation and to the number of people you have doing the actual cleaning.

A Sample System

The system that we use is as follows: We have one person who takes care of emptying the garbage and ash trays, one person who takes care of dusting the desks, one person who vacuums the carpets and one person who sweeps (dust mops) the non-carpeted floors. We have the person who does the garbage and ash trays usually one desk or one office ahead of the person doing the dusting. This allows time for any dust to settle as a result of the garbage and ash trays being emptied.

Whoever is finished their job first then cleans the washrooms and the front glass doors. Usually the person who sweeps (dust mops) the non-carpeted floors, when finished, then cleans the washrooms. In many offices the amount of floor to be swept is small.

This will allow that person time to clean and service the washrooms. And usually the person, who empties the garbage, when finished cleans the front doors of finger marks and damp mops the front tile entrance, if applicable. Vacuuming and dusting will usually take longer than doing the garbage and the sweeping.

This system, as explained above, can be used if you have more than one person involved in the cleaning. However, if there is only one or two people involved in the cleaning then there still needs to be a system as described above, but with some variations. The garbage stills needs to be done before the dusting. If only one person is doing the work, then that person will begin by doing the garbage and in a systematic manner, will go around the exterior private offices emptying the garbage bins and ashtrays and damp wiping them.

After all the garbage in the side or private offices has been taken care of, he will then empty the garbage and ash trays in the general office areas. Once all the garbage is emptied, then he can empty the garbage in the washrooms and lunch area, if applicable. Take note that if it is a one person operation, this is not the time to clean and service the washroom.

It is important to stay in a system and this part of the system is emptying the garbage. This system will save you much time and energy. The idea here is to "completely" finish all the garbage before going on to the next job.

Again, for a one person operation, once the garbage is completed then the next job will be the dusting of the desks. Keeping within your system, begin with the side or private offices, doing each one completely and moving onto the next.

After this is completed then move on into the general office area and complete this. The reason why the dusting is done before the carpets are vacuumed is because generally when dusting, some dust, crumbs and such will invariably end up on the carpet or tile floors.

Doing the vacuuming "after" the dusting is best and saves doing the same job twice or having to go back and pick up things that were dusted off the desks.

Once the garbage and dusting is completed the next job will be to dust mop the non-carpeted floors. Next will be the vacuuming. The reason for the vacuuming to be almost the last thing done is because anything that has found its way to the carpet as a result of the previous cleaning operations can now be vacuumed up and a nice clean carpet will meet your clients in the morning.

Again, remember your system. Use the same routine that you did with the dusting and garbage. It will save you time and prevent rooms or areas being missed. After the vacuuming is completed, clean and service the washrooms. After that you can then clean the front doors. And finally, damp mop the front entrance tile floor and spot damp mop the washroom floors, if needed.

If your client has a lunch room you may need to spot damp mop around the coffee area or other small areas on the floor - that is of course if the floor is a non-carpeted floor.

As mentioned above, using and keeping a system is vitally important, but also remember the important reasons as to why there is an order in which the various cleaning operations are done. This will save you time and money. This will allow you to get in and get out quickly and yet provide a first class service for your client.

Vinyl Window Blinds

Depending on where you live, chances are that the offices you will clean will not have vertical or horizontal mini blinds. Generally, they are used for residential purposes or even some institutional situations. However, if the office that you are cleaning does have these kinds of blinds on the windows – it would be good to address it here. Usually blind cleaning is considered an additional service because of the time needed to do a job that will satisfy your client.

A general, light dusting of these blinds can be done by using a "Swiffer type" duster that has a dust magnet chemical on it. You would completely close the blinds and then simply run the duster over the one side of the blinds. Then you would open the blinds fully until the other side of the blinds is exposed and then run the duster again over them.

Remember this is only a light dusting. This should be done before any other dusting is done in the office to avoid unwanted dust settling on the desk, counters, etc., and being missed.

If your client desires to have the blinds thoroughly cleaned you can either choose to do them yourself or have a different company come in and do them. Complete blind cleaning is something that we have never had to do and thus is not within the scope of this book.

Usually, unless the blinds are of very high quality, it really doesn't pay to have them professionally cleaned. If the blinds are old you could run into broken ropes and discoloration of the blind elements. We have found in many cases it was more cost efficient to buy new blinds.

Carpets: Some Helpful Tips

When vacuuming carpets it is not always necessary to vacuum every last square inch of carpet. On a nightly cleaning job concentrate mostly on the main traffic areas and under the knee hole part of the desks where people put their feet, as well as the front and back entrances into the office.

As a rule people don't walk on every square inch of carpet in the office. As you are vacuuming keep an eye on the surrounding areas for paper clips, staples, and other items that need to be vacuumed. However, this does not mean that you neglect the other areas. Monitor these other areas by vacuuming them weekly or as required to keep them looking clean.

Again, establish a system for the vacuuming and stick to it. A small magnet will lift up paper clips, and dry ice will help to remove gum.

Keep an eye on the edges of the carpet that are along the wall or partitions. These areas will occasionally, usually once a week, need a touching up. The easiest way we have found to do this is to use a small sized Wisk broom. Go around the edges with the Wisk broom and use a brushing motion towards the center of the carpet. This will allow you to remove any fluff and dust in those areas. This is best to be done before the vacuuming and thus will allow you to vacuum any fluff or dust that is removed from the edges.

Carpeted Stairs

If the office that you are cleaning has carpeted stairs you have a couple of options for vacuuming these stairs.

You could use your regular vacuum to vacuum the stairs. We have found this to be somewhat awkward and depending on the number of stairs involved – can tire or strain your back. This method does work though.

What we have found to be most useful is to purchase a small handheld vacuum cleaner. We have used both Hoover and Dirt Devil. We always make sure that they are the handheld vacuums that contain a cloth bag and have motor driven brushes. This is a great time saver and does a really great job. This kind of handheld vacuum can be purchased at your local Janitorial Supply House or sometimes at the local Wal-Mart.

You don't need to go out and spend hundreds and hundreds of dollars on a fancy handheld vacuum. If you observe the guidelines above it will more than meet your needs.

22

CARPET CLEANING

Carpet cleaning is another area of the business that you will need to decide whether or not you will do it. We don't try to generate carpet cleaning business. We are happy with just regular office cleaning. But from time to time we have been asked to clean a client's carpet. See the section below that explains what you should consider if asked to clean a carpet.

However, having said that if your desire is to diversify and bring in some addition monies, then carpet cleaning might be something you will want to consider. One of the advantages of having regular cleaning contracts is that when they need their carpets cleaned you are already in the building and have the overall cleaning contract. This model is an easy way to expand your business.

However, if you decide to not do carpet cleaning we have given you some further thoughts in this chapter.

Spots & Spills

In your normal day to day or week to week cleaning there will be times when you will have to remove spots or spilled coffee from your client's carpets. If the spots are minor and take only a minute or two to clean we don't charge our client.

Actually this is a good selling point for your services. But on the other hand if the traffic area of the carpet or the entire carpet is considerably soiled and the client requests it to be cleaned - then of course we charge them extra for this service. In our case, for most of our clients, carpet cleaning is not included as a regular service in the Service Outline, but is considered an additional service and therefore is invoiced separately.

For our clients who request that regular carpet cleaning be included in the regular cleaning schedule; we charge them by the square foot. Multiply this by the number of times per year they have requested their carpet to be cleaned and then divide the total by twelve. This in turn gives us a monthly charge.

Some clients may request their carpets cleaned every 6 or 12 months. You could arrange with them to invoice them separately after the completion of each carpet cleaning or put it into the monthly billing cycle as explained above. We personally don't include the carpet cleaning in the monthly billing cycle, but rather bill it as an additional service - even though the carpet cleaning would be scheduled to be cleaned on a regular basis.

Below is a method we have used for years that gives us an estimate of the carpet cleaning job.

FOR EXAMPLE:

10,000 sq. ft. (carpeted area)

X .20 (20 cents per sq. ft.-* see below for explanation)

=$ sub cost X 1 (times per year carpet to be cleaned)

= $ cost/per year

divided by 12

= $ per/month (for 12 months).

NOTE: The dirtier the carpet and the nature of the dirt will determine how much and the type of cleaning chemicals you will need. If the dirt on the carpet is oil then a degreaser is needed which is more costly than regular cleaning fluid.

If a carpet is covered with oil it will also take you longer to clean that carpet. Take this into consideration when pricing. If the traffic area of the carpet is heavily soiled you will need what is called a "traffic area spot cleaner" (obtained from your local Janitorial Supply House). If you need to purchase "traffic spot cleaner" you will need to take the cost of this into consideration when pricing the job.

This is another reason why we have learned over the years to stay with straight commercial cleaning contracts rather than industrial contracts. Heavy continuous carpet cleaning can throw you off your schedule and mess up your plans. Don't forget that you will need to have a life outside of your cleaning business. You will want to have time to do those things that you would not normally be able to do if you just simply worked for someone else.

Some Choices To Consider - If Asked:

If you are asked to clean a carpet, there are basically three avenues available for you to consider:

1. You can subcontract it out to a professional carpet cleaner
2. You clean it
3. Tell your client you don't have the equipment to do the job

If You Subcontract

If you don't feel comfortable cleaning carpets, that is not a problem. Just look in the Yellow Pages and locate a carpet cleaning specialist that is not in the office cleaning business as well. The fact that the carpet cleaning person is not also in the cleaning business is a very important consideration.

When you look in the Yellow Pages look for the people who do not have Janitorial Service and Carpet Cleaning. When you call a possible carpet cleaning company, before you tell him who you are and what you want, find out if he does regular office cleaning as well as carpet cleaning. You don't want to give your competition any inside opportunities.

You can also ask him how much he generally charges for a carpet cleaning job. You may need to describe the type of carpet and the setting in which it is in. More than likely he will say that he can't give a firm estimate unless he sees the carpet. This is normal. Before you invite him to see the carpet you can ask him some other questions like - how long has he been in business, etc.

If you feel comfortable with him, you can then arrange to meet him after your client is closed, so he can give you an estimate in writing. It is important to get it in writing and find out if he has any guarantees in terms of spot removal etc.

Make sure that he has proper liability insurance and bonding. This is just a simple question you can ask and he should not have a problem with the question. You don't want to be responsible if he breaks something or even steals something. This has never happened in all the years we've been in cleaning. Don't forget this is a service to "your" client. You are the one who will save your client the bother of doing all of this. It is a service that you will get paid to do.

After obtaining his written quotation, which will include any guarantees, you then add an administration charge (usually 10% of his total price) on top of his price and present this new price to "your" client for his approval. It is not necessary for you to tell your client who is going to do the carpet cleaning.

In reality, most of the time your client won't care just as long as the carpet is done well. Usually a quick call to your client with the price will be good and more than likely you will get an immediate answer - usually in the affirmative. We have found that the only time the answer was not immediate was when the carpet cleaning job was quite large and involved a considerable sum of money. Our client needed to get approval from his sources before he could give us the go-ahead. In this situation the approval only took a day or so to get.

Your client might ask for you to put your new carpet cleaning price in writing and give it to them. This is not a problem. Just use your letterhead and outline the carpet cleaning job with the price. See the sample in this book.

Once you get the okay, then contact the carpet cleaner and make the necessary arrangements for him to clean the carpets after your client's office hours. You will need to open the doors for the carpet cleaning company and then go back and lock them up again after the job is completed. We "never" gave an outside contractor of any kind keys to our client's office. This is one of the unspoken rules of the cleaning business.

This sounds like it is complicated, but really it's a breeze. For a little bit of leg work and a couple of phone calls you can make 10% profit - for doing very little.

If You Decide To Do It Yourself

If you decide to clean the carpet yourself you can rent the carpet cleaning machine needed to do the job from a local "Equipment Rental Company". Sometimes Janitorial Supply Houses also rent them as well. We have found that it is better to rent one from the equipment rental company rather than the Janitorial Supply House. The machines from the equipment rental company are usually in better condition.

Whichever source you choose, make sure that you get quality equipment that has been well maintained. If the machine you are going to rent looks beat up, then chances are that it won't work well and you will waste a lot of time.

To avoid this, make sure that the machine is clean looking inside and out and that there are no dents in the parts of the machine. Have a quick look at the hoses. If the hoses are frayed or in rough shape you could find yourself in difficulties in the middle of the job. Trust me. We have been there, done that, and in the process wasted a lot of time. Over the years we put into practice what I have just said above and found it to be a life saver.

We have found that the best kind of carpet cleaning machine is called the "Steam Cleaning" or "Hot Water Extraction" cleaning machine. This type of carpet cleaner sprays a fine spray of hot water and cleaning solution onto the carpet and then by moving the wand - extracts the dirty water from the carpet. There are also machines available through some local supermarkets.

However it is important that you be very picky if you decide to go this route. The machine must be in excellent condition or even new if possible. These machines can sometimes be abused and you could end up with a lemon.

If You Decide To Not Handle It At All

If you decide not to get involved in carpet cleaning at all you can simply tell your client that you just do not have the equipment that would result in a professional job. Most clients will understand and call a carpet cleaner on their own. You may want to recommend a carpet cleaner that again, is not in the Janitorial business as well.

However, you do provide a service. We have found that if we don't want to do the carpet cleaning ourselves we simply subcontract it out. In all the years we have done cleaning, we have never given the option to the client for them to go out and get their own carpet cleaner.

Although we have cleaned many carpets and large areas of carpets, most of the time we just subcontracted it out to another carpet cleaning company. When we have gone this route, our client has been satisfied, we didn't have to do the work, and we even picked up a 10% commission for doing almost nothing.

FLOOR CARE - PART 1
HOW TO MAINTAIN YOUR CLIENT'S FLOORS

Introduction (non-carpeted floors)

Although this section will deal with non-carpeted floor care, I think it is good to insert some interesting information that might be of help. In our own experience in being selective in the type of cleaning contracts we have obtained, we have found that offices that had ceramic type tile, glazed brick, and marble, finished stone or similar were the easiest to maintain.

You do not generally need to put any floor finish on these types of floors and a simple damp mopping removes dirt and soil. These types of floors are very easy to clean and keep clean.

However, when you begin your cleaning business you may decide not to be as selective as we have been and decide to take on cleaning contracts that have a certain amount of regular flooring such as, tile, linoleum and similar. In that case, the information below will be helpful for you.

Regular floor maintenance is not difficult. It involves sweeping the floor area with a treated dust mop, damp mopping the floor when necessary to remove coffee spills, oil, and dirt as needed and then dry buffing or spray buffing the main traffic areas - usually once weekly.

Spray Buffing Explained.

Spray buffing is buffing the floor with a floor buffing machine using a red spray buffing pad. The "spray" of spray buffing is a technique used to quickly remove scuff marks and black heel marks from your floors. This assumes that the floor already has some floor finish on it (it's shiny).

A floor buffing machine is also called a "Swing" buffing machine and is very easy to use. It is called a swing machine because it will move from right to left or left to right buffing the floor.

The direction the floor buffing machine goes is determined by you either lifting or dropping the handle. It only takes a few minutes to get the hang of it. Basically, when the floor buffer is running - that is, it is turned on and you are holding the handles; a slight lifting of the handle up will cause the buffer to go in the left direction, while a slight lowering of the handle will cause it to go to the right. Holding the handles level will keep the buffer on the same spot. This is so easy that we have seen children using these machines with ease.

To begin the process of spray buffing, begin by filling approximately one third of a 16 oz. handheld spray bottle with pure floor finish and fill the remainder two thirds with cold water. Your local Janitorial Supply House has these bottles. They can come in different sizes but the 16 oz. is the industry standard. They are very reasonably priced.

As you buff the floor with the floor machine using a red spray buffing pad, spray a fine mist or a small stream of the diluted floor finish on the area you wish to buff. Do not spray a large area of the floor, but rather a small area of a couple of tiles at a time. We have used both the "tan" and "red" spray buffing pad.

If we found that the tan pad wasn't cleaning the floor and removing the scuff marks we would then use the red pad. Usually, the red pad will do the trick.

The spray buffing pad will spread the solution that you have sprayed on the floor area and then dry it up quickly and in the process, due to friction and heat, will remove the scuff marks, heel marks and leave a shiny "baked on look" on the floor.

With spray buffing, remember to buff the floor in sections. Don't spray too much of the floor at one time. Spray only the area that you will immediately buff. In most cases when you spray buff you only need a little spray at a time. If you spray too much of the solution on the floor at one time it will clog up your buffing pad and you won't get the results you desired. Only spray the solution when and where you want to improve the visual appearance of the floor.

If you have damp mopped the floor before you spray buff, wait until the floor is completely dry before spray buffing. If you start spray buffing while the floor is still wet you will compromise the finish and create a lot of work for yourself.

If the floor is dirty, you can damp mop it prior to buffing or use a little more spray, but use the spray only a little at a time. The dirt from the floor will go into the buffing pad and will clog it up quickly.

On occasion, we have used as much as a 50/50 solution in the spray buffing bottle. That is 50% cold water and 50% floor finish. This type of solution would only be used when the floor needs more than just a quick light touch up.

You will find that the higher the percentage of the mixture the faster your buffing pad will fill up and clog. If the pad clogs just turn it over and use the other side. If the floor is fairly dirty it would be easier to damp mop it first. We don't use any of the commercial "spray buff" solutions because we have found that many of them can cause the floor to be slippery.

As already mentioned above, we just use cold water and a percentage of the floor finish. We use cold water in the mixture rather than warm or hot water. Cold water will give you a better result.

When spray buffing, remember to just spray buff the traffic areas where the people walk. It is not necessary to spray buff right up to the baseboards.

Basically, that is all there is to it. In some cases we have found that it is not necessary to damp mop the floor before spray buffing, which in turn saves us time. This would of course depend on the type of office, weather conditions, and so on.

The floor machine that you will use for spray buffing is just a standard buffer. We use a high speed buffer that runs at 300 rpm. As we have already mentioned previously, it can be either purchased or rented as needed. However, the discs or pads that you will use for buffing, scrubbing or stripping the floors will need to be purchased. The pads can be used over and over again and will last a long time.

If you find later that the floor is not responding to spray buffing and is not as shiny as it once was, and the floor seems to scuff up faster with black heel marks, then the solution would be to re-coat the floor.

Re-coating the floor can be accomplished by spray buffing with a 50/50 solution, as described above using a red buffing pad. If the floor is dirty you can use a blue spray clean pad. Usually the red pad does the job.

After spray buffing the floor, sweep the floor, using your commercial dust mop, to remove any powder and loose. After this apply one or two thin coats of floor finish on the main traffic areas only. Use a 16 oz. string mop to do this. Stay about 2-4 inches (about ½ a tile) from the edges. Allow plenty of time to dry; hopefully 24 hours to cure.

After this, simply maintain the floor by spray buffing as noted above. This re-coating will also be further discussed later in this book.

When washing a floor that has floor finish applied to it, never use harsh floor cleaning chemicals or hot water. The hot water will soften the floor finish and the harsh chemicals will break down the finish and cause problems later on down the road. Use a **neutral non scum detergent** and either cold or lukewarm water.

You can obtain the neutral non scum detergent from your local Janitorial Supply House, but be sure to specify that it is "neutral non scum detergent." This is very important.

Here is a video to illustrate spray buffing: View here https://goo.gl/1LmiKs

Another Method of Buffing - High Speed Burnishing

Another way of buffing a floor is using what is called the "burnishing method." The burnishing method uses a high speed, or as some call it, an ultra-high speed buffer. This buffer is not a swing machine/buffer as previous mentioned above, but is a high speed Burnisher that has wheels at the back and you simply push it forward or backward effortlessly over the floor.

A burnishing machine can be purchased new or used and even some equipment rental companies might have them available for rent. In the burnishing method only a small part of the high speed buffing pad is in contact with the floor. This Burnishing machine operates at high speeds - up to 1000 rpm and some are even a little faster.

This Burnisher works in conjunction with special floor finishes designed to work with the high speed Burnisher and the heat/friction caused by the Burnisher. You can obtain this special burnishing floor finish from your local Janitorial Supply House. Most regular floor finishes will not stand up to this type of high speed burnishing.

This burnishing method is excellent. It gets the job done much faster and much easier than regular spray buffing. The results of the burnishing method will give a much deeper shine that will stand up to much more traffic, last longer and will be much easier to maintain.

This is the same method many cleaning companies use when cleaning large grocery stores.

To use the burnishing method of floor care here is a suggested plan. Sweep the floor that you will be burnishing with a treated dust mop to remove any dust and loose dirt. Begin by damp mopping the floor with clear cold water to remove any coffee stains, etc. Then let the floor completely dry. Now, run the Burnisher over the floor with the buffing pad - usually a white pad and you will see the results.

Although some cleaners, at times, spray a very fine mist of clear cold water on areas of the floor to simulate spray buffing, most cleaning companies don't - they just burnish the floor without any water. Of course with this method it is understood that the floor finish that you will be buffing will be the special floor finish designed for burnishing.

When the time comes that you need to re-coat the main traffic areas use the guidelines already outlined for re-coating. The only difference is that you will now be using the floor finish for burnishing. If you are going to strip or scrub a floor and you intend to use the burnishing method to maintain that floor, then you can substitute the regular floor finish with the floor finish that is designed for burnishing.

This burnishing method will cost you a little more in materials , but the costs are well worth it. It does provide an excellent end result and many cleaning companies are going this route, even in small offices. The burnishing method is only used on floors that you would normally apply floor finish to and not floors that would be ceramic tile or the like. Keep in mind that you don't need to use the burnishing method, but if you decide to go that route you will be pleased with the end results and so will your clients.

Here is a video to illustrate burnishing: View here https://goo.gl/HyLcTU

NOTE: As mentioned previously, you can be very picky as to the type of cleaning contracts you go after. If you want to be picky and choose offices that only have a minimal amount of tile flooring to maintain, but mostly carpet, then that is a good way to go.

This is our first choice. It saves us a lot of time, effort and equipment. You are the boss. You can be as picky as you want. And while you are considering being picky, the type of floors your potential client has should be considered. Ceramic tiles and marble floors are much easier to clean and maintain than vinyl tile flooring.

24

FLOOR CARE - PART 2
STRIPPING AND REFINISHING

If you take over a new contract and there is tile that has been poorly taken care of or if weather conditions (salt, ice, etc.) have caused the floor condition to deteriorate, then there may come a time when you will need to strip the floor and refinish it. Stripping a floor means to completely remove all the old floor finish and then re-coat it with new floor finish.

Stripping floors is only done when absolutely necessary. We have had offices where we have never had to strip the floors. Simple spray buffing maintained them nicely. When we have acquired a new contract where the previous cleaners did not take care of the tile floors and we have found it necessary to strip the floors - we have sometimes charged the new client a "clean up" charge.

Other times we have just thrown it in as a "good faith" gesture. Which course of action we have taken has been determined by the size of the floor area that needed to be stripped. If the area was small, then more than likely we have done it for free.

If the area was large we have charged for the service. We have had to just play it by ear. But there may come a time when you will have to strip and refinish a floor, and this next section will explain how to do this.

As mentioned above, stripping a floor is simply removing all the old wax (floor finish) using a floor machine (slow speed - 175 rpm) with a brown or black stripping pad, together with the appropriate wax stripping chemical - available through any Janitorial supply house.

The different colored floor pads can be purchased separately. Each different color designates a specific usage. For example: A red floor pad is considered a spray buff pad while a blue pad is considered a spray clean pad. The green pad is used for scrubbing or heavy spray cleaning - usually used in industrial type offices. The black and brown pads are used for stripping. Another pad that we use is the white pad which is good for obtaining a higher gloss shine on marble and tile floors.

When the pads get dirty they can be washed just like clothing. Just throw them in a washing machine - no soap is needed and then dry them in the dryer. Alternatively, you can wash them and rinse them in a laundry tub and then let them drip dry. Unless you hit a metal object while using them they will last for a while.

How To Tell If A Floor Needs Refinishing

To determine if a floor needs to be stripped and refinished you examine the edges and the main traffic areas. If the edges are darker in color (brown or black) compared to the rest of the floor then usually stripping is required. Although, under certain conditions, the edges could be stripped separately without necessitating the entire floor being stripped, we have found that usually the difference of the newly stripped edges and the rest of the floor is too great a difference to leave.

Also if the main traffic areas of the floor are a lighter color than the rest (by this we mean that you can clearly see the walking path on the floor as the floor finish is being walked off), this would indicate that stripping of the floor would be necessary.

On many occasions, if there was only a slight difference between the center walking are of the floor and the edges or other areas - we have just spray cleaned the center with a blue pad and re-coated that area with two or three thin coats of floor finish. The result hs been great and has lasted for a long time.

Floor Stripping Only As A Last Result

We have found that stripping should be done only as a last resort. It is not hard, but it does take time to properly strip a floor and refinish it. Scrubbing is another alternative. Scrubbing is accomplished in the same manner as stripping, but scrubbing does not remove all the old floor finish. Scrubbing removes embedded dirt, and allows you to re-coat the floor for a great look. You would use a green floor pad to scrub. On occasion when the floor has only required a light scrubbing we have used a blue floor pad and even a red floor pad.

How To Strip A Floor:

To strip or scrub a floor you will need to obtain the proper chemicals from your local Janitorial supply house. Read and follow the directions on the container. Select the proper colored pad for the job - black for stripping and green for scrubbing. See note above regarding other colored pads.

When scrubbing a floor most of the time you only need a general purpose floor cleaner. You only want to remove ingrained dirt and then re-coat the floor. To strip the floor you will need a stripper chemical to remove the old floor finish. When actually doing the job make sure all cords, waste baskets and chairs, are removed from the floor.

Picture the floor in your mind's eye and divide it into sections. Do not begin stripping or scrubbing too large a section at a time. Many people make this mistake and the floor dries too quickly and takes longer to do. Instead start with a smaller section of the floor - a workable section.

We find that a workable section would be 5 feet by 5 feet. Soak the floor (don't flood it - there is a difference) and let the solution stay on the floor for about 5-10 minutes. After this, run the floor machine with the appropriate pad, over the floor section, tile row by tile row, until the floor is visibly clean. You may have to run the floor machine over the same row of tiles several times to clean them.

After stripping this section of floor, dry it up using the mop pail and wringer. Sometimes we have used a "wet vacuum" with a squeegee attachment to remove the dirty water. This does a great job and is faster. Removing the dirty water will allow you to see how clean the floor actually is. Re-soak another area of the floor and do the same procedure again until the entire floor is completed.

Helpful Hints

Be careful in offices where carpets meet the tiled flooring that you are stripping. If strong stripping chemicals are allowed to spread freely on the carpet, fading or spotting may occur. Usually a good rule of thumb is to stay about 3 inches from the baseboards and carpets. These 3 inches can easily be cleaned by hand using a hand held pad for the job.

There are a number of edge-cleaning tools available. These tools make it very easy to clean the edges without causing your back to become tired. An edge cleaner is a small pad holder on a swivel with a convenient pole attached. It is used for cleaning edges and corners from a standing position - which saves you bending down. These can be purchased at your local Janitorial Supply House. We have used these edge cleaners for years and they work great. However, we have also used the removable center part of the stripping/scrubbing pad to do the same by hand.

By the way, there are also different chemicals available which liquefy the old floor wax (floor finish). The chemicals return the old floor finish to its original liquid state. We have used these products with great success. They save time and money.

We have found using this type of chemical gets the job done very well in a fraction of the normal time. They save time and labor even though they cost slightly more than the conventional stripping chemicals. We have found that they not only save us a great deal of time but are very easy to use. Some of these products even boast about doing the job without having to use a floor machine at all.

After the floor is completely stripped and dried, examine it for any spots or missed areas. If there is any touching up required, do it at this time.

Here is a video to illustrate stripping a floor: https://goo.gl/EAD4kH

How To Rinse The Floor After Stripping It:

Now, if you are happy with the results of your work, the next step is to rinse the floor with clear cold water. Rinsing is simply rewetting the floor and mopping it up again. You can either use clear cold water or you can add a little white vinegar (about 2 oz. per pail). This removes any soap film and alkaline from the floor and prepares the floor to be sealed.

Make sure that the mop you use to rinse is absolutely clean. We use a different mop to rinse the floor rather than using the mop we used to strip the floor with. Again, usually a 16 oz. string mop will do.

Here is a video to illustrate rinsing a floor after stripping: https://goo.gl/cBsosr

Should You Use A Sealer?

When the floor is rinsed and completely dry, you are now ready to refinish. At this point we apply 2 coats of sealer. However, not all Janitorial companies will do this. The reason we do this is because it gives a firm base for the floor finish, which in turn, results in a better looking job which lasts longer and is easier to maintain.

If you choose to seal your floors, choose a sealer for the appropriate type of flooring you are working with. There are different sealers on the market for terrazzo and tile. Get the right one. Don't use a sealer that is labeled specifically only for terrazzo and then use it on tile - it may damage the tile.

However, there are some excellent sealers that can be used as a multi-purpose sealer for different kinds of flooring. Consult with your local Janitorial Supply house as to what they have in terms of a general purpose sealer. Depending on where you live and the weather conditions, it would be good to ask the representative what most cleaning companies use in your area. The Janitorial Supply House representatives generally know their products.

Keep in mind though - that you don't need to buy the most expensive product they have. If you decide to use a sealer just get the general purpose one that suits your needs. No glitter or glamour. You don't need a sealer that would survive an explosion.

Here is a thought: When considering whether or not to use a sealer; if the floor you're working on is porous; that is, it seems to soak up the water quickly, then using a sealer is a recommended step to obtain good results. Rubber tile and battleship linoleum seem to have this characteristic. If the floor is excessively porous you may wish to apply 3 coats of sealer.

How to Seal The Floor:

Applying sealer to a floor is quite easy. Make sure that the floor is clean and free of any powder and dirt. Use a clean, very slightly damp mop for applying the sealer. Simply put the clean string mop into a bucket, pour the sealer over the mop and then wring the mop out until the excess sealer is removed. The mop should be wet but not dripping with the sealer. Then apply the sealer to the floor similar to how you would wash the floor. When the mop is no longer "evenly" covering the floor with sealer apply more sealer to the mop as stated above.

When you are applying the sealer to the floor make sure that the tiles you are sealing are completely covered with the sealer with no missed spots. In other words, that there are no areas of the tile that are wet with sealer and other areas that are dry or not covered. The entire set of tiles or section of floor you are working on needs to be completely covered with sealer.

When applying the sealer section by section, when you come to the edge of each section use the mop to make a straight line as to where that section begins or ends. When you do other sections and then join up with these sections you have completed, you will have a clear mark to know where to go and where to stop.

We have found that simply pouring the sealer on the mop while the mop is sitting on the floor seems to be much faster and saves the sealer from being wasted. Use the mop to spread the sealer over the floor, but again spread the sealer in sections - as already mentioned.

Don't try to cover too large an area with the sealer at any given time. If you try to do too large an area at one time you will find that when the sealer dries or partially dries, you will have difficulties with overlapping. It is better to do smaller areas at a time. Again, the important part of applying sealer is that you apply it evenly, being very careful not to miss any tiles.

The first coat of sealer should be applied from baseboard to baseboard. The second coat should be applied basically to the heavy traffic areas only. Make sure that you allow plenty of time for drying between coats, otherwise the first coat will blotch. When applying the sealer just apply thin coats not heavy coats. Remember, two thin coats are better than one thick coat.

We have found that using, what is called, a tied mop, for applying both sealer and floor finish is the best way to go. A tied mop is just a mop that has a strand of mop string on the very ends of the mop strands that hold the mop strands in place. This makes for a much easier application of floor finishes and sealers. Many cleaning companies use these kinds of string mops for general mopping as well.

Alternative to sealer:

Some companies prefer to apply an additional coat of floor finish (wax) rather than going through the process of sealing the floor. In some cases this works well, we have done this also. However; we have found that the appearance and care of the floor is better and easier if sealer is used. But like I said, many companies go the extra coat of finish route rather than dealing with sealer. You can make the decision.

How To Apply Floor Finish To The Floor:

Waxing or applying the floor finish is basically the same as applying the sealer. The floor finish is like the finish coat and is the last chemical put on the floor. The instruction for applying floor finish is almost the same as applying sealer. Use a string mop and wet it with the wax (not soak) and spread the wax over the floor evenly using the mop in sections making sure that you don't miss any areas.

After the first coat is applied wait until the floor is dry and apply the second coat. The second coat is usually applied to the main traffic areas and usually about 2-4 inches from the baseboard.

We have found that the first coat takes longer to dry than the second coat. This drying time will vary according to your location and the season of the year. If you have decided not to seal the floor then after the second coat of floor finish has dried you may wish to apply a third coat but, again only in the main walking areas. After the stripping and refinishing process is completed, the floor can be maintained by the floor maintenance program of spray buffing.

NOTE: Just a couple of helpful hints regarding waxing and sealing of floors: Make sure that chairs and waste baskets are removed from the floor. If they make a mark on the wax or sealer when wet and then allowed to dry, the mark will remain. Floor finish is best after it has been allowed at least 24 hours to harden.

If you are planning to strip and refinish a floor or even simply re-coat a floor, try to schedule it to be done on a day that will allow the floor at least 24 hours to dry without any traffic. Also be sure to allow plenty of time for each coat of sealer/wax to dry before applying another coat.

The product manufacturer will more than likely tell you the drying time required. If you find that the floor seems to be taking forever to dry, the problem may be a result of a lack of air circulation. Simply open a door or use a fan to cause air circulation enabling the floor to dry faster.

In some instances when we clean vaults and elevators in banks and office buildings we try to bring an electric fan which moves the air and dries the floors faster. This works great! Remember, our goal is to get in and get out fast while doing an excellent job.

See the video illustration link above under the heading stripping. This video also gives an illustration of how to apply floor finish.

What type of Floor Finish should you use?

Your local Janitorial Supply House will carry different floor finishes. We have found that Johnston & Johnston "commercial" floor finishes are good products. In some cases they tend to be a little more expensive but will more than pay for themselves in the long run. Dustbane products are also good products. You would need to check, Dustbane products might only be available in some locations.

NOTE: AVOID using off the shelf "domestic" floor waxes from supermarkets. We have found that they will only bring grief in the long run. Use only "commercial" floor finishes.

Also - if you are planning on maintaining the floor(s) using the **burnishing method** as described above - then the floor finish you will choose **will be different** from regular floor finish. It will be floor finish specially designed for burnishing. In some cases you may not need a sealer.

Always read the label and directions for application on floor finish containers especially floor finish designed for burnishing. It will save you time and money by following the instructions carefully.

For the most part we use what is called a "high gloss metallic cross linked" floor finish. This type of floor finish might be called something different in various parts of the country. It generally contains 12-16% solids. Just because a floor finish has a higher solids content doesn't mean that it's a better floor finish.

Many of our clients desire a high gloss or shine on their non-carpeted floors and thus the reason for the high gloss finish. However, when the shininess of the floor is not an issue we use a "low shine" floor finish. This is MUCH easier to maintain and can cost you less in the long run.

A low shine floor finish does not show the scuff marks as much as a high gloss finish will. The floor will not need as much spray buffing to keep it looking nice. Remember, the higher the gloss the more it will show marks and scuffing and will require more maintenance to keep it looking good.

How To Re-Coat A Floor:

We have mentioned the term "re-coating" in various places in this book, but I thought it might be good to gather those thoughts and bring them into one specific section for reference purposes.

Re-coating a floor is needed when you can visibly see a difference in the main traffic areas of a floor and in the low traffic areas. You will begin to see that the floor finish is beginning to wear off. To re-coat you will need to make sure that the floor is clean and free of any dirt.

Depending on the condition of the floor; many times just giving the floor a good spray buffing in the main traffic areas with a 50/50 spray solution of finish will suffice. You will then, again, sweep the floor with a treated dust mop to remove any powder that will be there as a result of the spray buffing.

At this point, on many occasions, after sweeping the floor, we have even taken a damp mop - wet with clear water- over the floor to make sure that any powder on the floor from spray buffing has been removed. We then simply re-coat the traffic areas with one or two "thin" layers of floor finish.

On other occasions where the floor looks "grungy" you might need to "lightly" scrub the areas by using a red pad and some cool water with a non-scum detergent. Typically, you would use a mop, pail and wringer to apply the water and mop up the floor.

With this type of "light" scrubbing you will not need to "soak" the floor, but rather just lightly wet it enough so it doesn't dry out on you while lightly scrubbing it. You will be using a regular slow speed buffer/scrubbing machine to do this. Do not use a high speed machine for this because it will spray the water everywhere.

It is best to not hover over any particular area of the floor with the machine, but just "glide" the machine across the floor from side to side. The same principles explained in the section about stripping in terms of only doing a section at a time will also apply here. Dry the floor with a mop and wait for the entire area to dry completely.

Once this is accomplished, carefully apply one or two coats of floor finish using the same method described in the section explaining how to apply floor finish. In this case you will only be re-coating the traffic areas and not the entire floor baseboard to baseboard.

Summary:

Strip floors using appropriate stripping chemicals and a black or brown disk. Mop the floor dry and then rinse with clear cold water. Allow to thoroughly dry. Apply two coats of sealer or three coats of floor finish. It's that simple.

How much to charge for stripping floors:

Different cleaning companies charge different amounts for this kind of work. There is no hard and fast rule or special formula. Your price will depend on where you are living and also the congestion of the area that is to be stripped.

There is a difference in terms of congestion of an empty auto show room and a tightly crowded office. A basic guideline that we have used for pricing stripping is to calculate the cost of the chemicals and supplies, take into consideration the amount of labor required and then add the profit we would like to make. This would give you a price. This price is just a guide and the charge may vary, again according to the type of job you are doing and the location of the job as well as the cost of materials needed to do the job.

If you are pricing an office where the tile floors have been much neglected and thus require stripping and refinishing, you might want to let the manager know that there will be a "floor refinishing" charge to restore the floor. However, if the tiled floor area is small we have absorbed the cost involved and just refinished it. We have even used this as a selling feature for our services and this works great! We have done this with some banks with a smaller customer entrance and waiting area. We have found that banks are excellent clients to have. They pay well and on time. Once you have one bank, it is easy to obtain other banks.

25

HOW TO DO WINDOW CLEANING

Window cleaning is generally a separate cleaning service and will be invoiced as an "additional service." However, it is understood that, as mentioned previously, the front entrance door glass is included in the regular cleaning and is reflected in the estimated cost of the regular cleaning.

The nightly cleaning of the front entrance doors is accomplished easily by using paper towels and a sprayer containing general glass cleaner. If your client's offices are to be cleaned on a once a week basis, then of course the front entrance doors would be cleaned weekly. However, on occasion you may be asked to clean a set of windows other than the entrance doors.

If there are only two or three windows; standard windows (not divided) on ground level, we have sometimes included them in the overall price at no additional cost. We have just stated that they will be cleaned "as required." This way we decide how often they get cleaned. If the office you are giving a price on is in a very dusty area or on a street that has major traffic, then the windows will need to be cleaned more often and this should reflect in your price.

However, if there are a number of windows that need to be cleaned regularly the going rate is about $2.00 per window per side per cleaning. Some cleaning services charge more per window side. This is for straightforward commercial windows - all glass and not multi framed sections to the window. This price is for office windows, not store windows. Office windows are usually about 3X5 or 4X6. Cleaning them is generally straight forward and very easy to do.

Store windows generally have signs and other advertising items that need to be either removed during cleaning or worked around. This will take time to do and needs to be reflected in your price.

With larger windows we charge more and if ladders are required, even more. Take into consideration the time larger windows would take you to do and how much your time is worth.

NOTE We have found that usually only the outsides of office windows need to be cleaned more regularly (monthly or as required). The insides need to be done considerably less often (sometimes only every 3-4 months) depending on how many people in the office smoke and the location of the office. With many places now being smoke free, this makes cleaning the inside windows easier.

Cleaning windows is relatively easy. Just wet the windows with a soapy solution using a window brush or a padded applicator. Make sure that the padded application pad is soft white and not anything that would scratch the glass. The soapy solution can be made up from a couple of drops of dish detergent in a bucket of warm water.

You don't need to go out and buy fancy window cleaning chemicals. We never have. We have found it to be a waste of time and money. Save your money. The best kind of dish soap to use is the yellow colored liquid dish soap.

After the windows are soaked use a squeegee in a top to bottom pattern (not from side to side) until the entire window has been cleaned. Be sure to wipe the rubber blade after each top to bottom pass. Purchase a professional squeegee from the Janitorial Supply House. It will be your best friend.

If you buy a dollar squeegee it will not do a proper job and will waste your time. Time is money. The professional squeegee will have replaceable rubber strips and does an excellent job. We have used larger squeegees, but generally use a 12" unit. This is adequate for most jobs.

For windows that might be out of your usual reach, a pole can be attached to the professional squeegee.

We have even used multi length extender poles with great success. When cleaning inside windows make sure to take care that water doesn't drip onto your client's papers or computers.

Want a faster method?

Another very fast, inexpensive method we have used with great success is to soap the outside windows with a soapy solution using a window brush and then hose or rinse them clean with a garden hose attached to a nearby faucet.

This method can only be used in selective circumstances. After hours is perhaps the best time to use this method to avoid people getting splashed. Of course it need not be said that this method cannot be used indoors, but rather the conventional method of squeegee use is the best for indoor window cleaning.

We used this method with a set of bank windows that were about 20 feet tall and about 5 feet off the ground. In this particular application it worked great.

A final note: Very small windows can be cleaned with a paper towel and glass cleaner.

26

HOW TO HANDLE COMPLAINTS

In all of our years we have had very few complaints. However, on occasion there may be a complaint from one of your customers. Knowing how to hand their complaint is very important. Customer relations are very important. If one of your clients calls with a complaint or inquiry, it is absolutely necessary to give them the impression that they are important to you.

When a client calls with a complaint, personal attention is needed. Listen to them carefully, assuring them that you will personally take care of the matter - and then do as you said. Don't be impatient with them or argumentative.

In keeping with he "personal" touch mentioned above, depending on the complaint it is usually a good idea to go and visit with your client and talk with him face to face. Even if the item he is complaining about is a small thing - your personal attention to the matter will speak volumes in terms of your reputation and customer service.

If a client calls and complains then this is a signal that this particular item is important to him. So, again, your personal attention to the matter will pay big dividends.

If perhaps the complaint is in connection with something that is not covered by your service outline then make an appointment to see them and discuss the matter. It may be that the price for your services may also have to be adjusted to take care of the new area of service.

27

STEPS TO PRICE INCREASES

If after you have cleaned an office for a short time and you realize that you have underpriced the services there are a couple of steps that you could take to correct the situation.

Three Steps to Consider

The First Step would be to examine your routine. Do you have a routine down pat which saves you time? Are you day dreaming while cleaning? If you have people helping you are they deliberately working slowly? In other words examine your own service and system of cleaning - can it be improved?

The Second Step would be to approach the management and explain to them that you have examined your own service and system and can't improve it to save time and money and therefore you must adjust your price. Usually, if you explain the situation to your client there is no problem.

However, taking over a contract and bidding purposely low, knowing that you will increase it later on is not ethical and will eventually come back to haunt you. In all the years that we have been in commercial office cleaning, there have only been a couple of times in which we needed to adjust our prices other than because of rising material and labor costs.

The need for you to increase your price might be as simple as keeping up with the cost of inflation and rising costs of materials. Business people understand this. If you have tried the first two methods without success than a third method may be in order.

The Third Step is to obtain another contract and cancel your services with the one that is no longer profitable. In all our years I can't remember a time that we have had to do this.

28

KEYS, SECURITY AND ALARM SYSTEMS

Keys

Because most of your cleaning will be done in the evening hours, that is, after hours, your client will give you a set of keys for his office. When you are given the keys in your hand, if your client doesn't try the keys in the door immediately, make sure that you do. Many times when a company is changing cleaning companies they also change the locks on their doors. On occasion these new keys do not work or just don't fit right. Try your set of keys to make sure they fit right and open the door.

Alarm Systems

Many offices across the country now have an alarm system installed. When your client gives you the keys to his office he will also give you instructions concerning the alarm system and sometimes a card with a special number on it. This card will provide proof that you or your employees are authorized to be in your client's building.

The alarm system is not something to be worried about. However, listen carefully to the instructions that your new client gives you regarding the alarm. Most alarms are very basic and almost use the same pattern to arm or disarm. It is not really a concern.

When you enter the premises to clean you will either turn the alarm off with a key or by punching in a three or four digit code number on the alarm control box. The only point to remember is to make sure to turn the alarm off within the designated grace time. This designated time is usually between 30-45 seconds after entering the office. If you miss this timing you may have a visit from the "boys in blue".

It is only good business relations to try to not cause false alarms for your client. By this I mean forgetting to turn off the alarm when entering the building which then ends up with a visit from the Police and or Alarm Company. "False alarms" could cost your client a fee.

If you clean a bank remember that they have panic buttons located usually at each teller's area and on some of the desks - usually the administration officer's desk and the manager's desk. When cleaning, the teller's area is usually not a problem but, be careful with the desks that may have a panic button. Pushing the chair under the knee hole area, in some cases, may accidentally set off the silent alarm. However, some alarm companies are changing the type of panic buttons used to ones that cannot be so easily accidentally set off.

Security

Because you will have the keys to your client's offices it is necessary that you make sure that all doors are closed and locked when leaving. If you notice any ground floor windows that are open or unlocked that could allow someone to gain entrance into the office, close and lock them also. When you enter your client's office lock the door behind you. This will prevent anyone from the street coming in to use the phone or the washroom. If you lock the door behind you, anyone entering the office has a key and therefore a right to be there.

If anyone comes to the door of the office and motions you to open the door, simply refuse and walk away. You don't have to open the door to anyone. If they have a right to be in the office they will have a key or will have made prior arrangements.

Who's In Charge?

Because of the importance of keys, alarm systems, and security, it is best that only one person, preferably the same person each night, be in charge of this responsibility. If the responsibility is given to different people mistakes can happen, doors can be left unlocked or alarm systems not put back on after leaving.

So if you have three people cleaning one office, put one in charge of security, keys, locking up and checking windows, etc. Incidentally, it is also a good idea that this same person, who is in charge of the keys, alarm systems, and the security also be in charge of ensuring that the proper lights be put off or left on after the cleaning is completed. Again, this procedure will help eliminate mistakes and thus keep your clients happy.

29

SELLING YOUR BUSINESS

There may come a time when you might wish to sell your cleaning business. Keep these things in mind.

Never tell any prospective purchaser either the name of a contract, the price of a contract or how long it takes you to do it. If you do you could lose your business. We made this mistake once years ago and lost contracts which, at that time, we couldn't afford to lose. We found that there are many people out there who want to get the name, price and details of your contracts for the sole purpose of stealing them from you. You need to take precautions.

When prospective clients approach you regarding purchasing your business simply have a printed sheet indicating how many contracts you have - remember no names, the approximate location of each (North end, East end, etc.), the payment of each, and the approximate time needed to clean each contract. This list with a list of equipment and expenses is all you need. You do not have to give them your company name either.

And it is not good to let a real estate company sell it for you. They will let your competitors know all your business. You can successfully do it yourself. We sold 4 cleaning businesses successfully this way and the new owners were very happy with them.

Arriving at a reasonable price for the sale of your business is not difficult. Many have come up with a price by multiplying the gross monthly income by 5; include the relative cost of equipment and goodwill and reputation. The resulting computation will be a nice figure for you.

30
HOW TO DEAL WITH TAXES

Like any other source of income there will be taxes need to be paid on the taxable amount. It is recommended that you keep good records of all your various income streams and your various expenses. These business expenses will need to be categorized detailing what each expense is for.

We have found it very beneficial to employ the services of a component bookkeeper. This bookkeeper should know the various tax laws, tax allowances and rules pertaining to your cleaning business. The cost of a good bookkeeper is usually very inexpensive and will save you the castle of trying to do it yourself. However, you will need to make that decision yourself.

31

HOW TO PREPARE THE SERVICE OUTLINE

We have discussed the "Service Outline" above. When you present your "Service Outline", that is, an outline of the services you will perform, it's important that it includes various details that you and your client have discussed and those which are standard in the cleaning. Below are the details, section by section, that we include in our "Service Outline."

Also see our sample "Service Outline" near the end of this eBook. In this section we will look at each part of the Service Outline.

Your client's name:

Just above the words "Service Outline" we type in our client's name, address, city, state/province, and zip/postal code. This makes the service outline more personal and tailor made just for them. This can be easily done on a computer with just about any word processor.

Cleaning equipment and supplies:

In your cleaning business you will supply all the materials needed to clean your client's office. The only exception might be that some banks supply the garbage bags. In our experience every bank we have cleaned has supplied the garbage bags. Most of them have purchased them through us.

Here is a useful tip regarding the garbage for banks. It will be very helpful to know this information. Many banks require their cleaning service to keep their paper garbage, in the bank basement or bank storage area, for 7-14 days. This is in case there is a deposit or accounting error they will be able to sift through the garbage to obtain information. When you put the garbage in the basement (or wherever the bank stores its garbage) you must label each day's garbage with the day of the week which clearly indicates which day's garbage is in each bag. It is important to keep kitchen garbage which contains coffee grinds and the like separate from the regular paper garbage. Put the kitchen garbage in a different garbage bag.

After the full week or 14 days you can then put the garbage out for the preceding time period at the next appointed garbage day. Check with the bank to find out how long they desire to keep the garbage. In your "Service Outline" for banks you will put in a small notation that indicates that you will hold the garbage for X number of days.

Let's get back to the Service Outline details.

The only products that your client is responsible for is the supply of washroom supplies: for example, toilet tissue, hand towels, hand soap, etc. If they wish, your client's can order these supplies through you, but they would be at an additional cost. Most of our clients order washroom supplies through us and we just bill them at the end of the month in addition to the regular invoice for cleaning. We also charge a 10% administration fee for providing the service of ordering, invoicing and paying for the washroom supplies. It is nice to make a 10% profit. Whatever the cost of the washroom supplies is we just add the 10% and present our client with the new total washroom supply price.

Time of Cleaning:

Your clients, in general, will not want you cleaning their offices during their business hours and you won't want to do it at that time either. In all the years that we have been cleaning, only two people have asked us to do it when they were open. Our policy is we only clean after hours. They will prefer you to do your work after they have closed. This is good because it will allow you to come and go as you please; thus setting your own hours.

Although some cleaning companies start at 4:30 p.m., the best time we have found to start is 7:00 p.m... If any of your clients work late they are usually gone by 7:00 p.m. However, set your own times that are best suited for you.

Frequency of Cleaning

Insert here the number of times per week you will clean your client's office. If it is a nightly service you will insert 5 nights a week. If it is a once or twice a week service you will insert the appropriate number. In all our years of cleaning we only had one contract that required a 6 day a week service.

Duties:

Here you will place a summary list of duties that you will perform in the course of your cleaning. It provides a quick reference and summary for your client to view and adjust to his satisfaction. If your client has mentioned something in particular that he would like to see done or something in particular that his present cleaners are missing, you could also insert this item here. You will also have the opportunity of pointing this out to him when both of you go over the Service Outline together.

Waste paper and litter:

Most clients have a means of disposing of garbage. Some may have a rental disposal bin while others will want you to put it out on the street for garbage collection. The client will pay for the disposal bin.

Waste Paper Bin Liners:

Waste paper bin liners usually need replaced periodically. Some cleaning companies rarely or never replace the waste paper liners in their client's offices. Many times this is a point of contention with managers. It is nice to come into a clean waste paper bin. If you decide to provide clean waste paper liners as required it would be an added advantage for you and your client. The cost for you to provide this benefit is pennies and can be a part of your overall pricing calculations. We always provide white liners. We have found that the black liners show the dirt more and require replacing more frequently.

Entrances and entrance doors:

Keeping your client's front entrance clean is an important point. During bad weather you may have to damp mop the front entrance floor area nightly or more frequently than normal. If the entrance is small we just use a 12 oz. deck mop and it does the job quick and easy. The glass doors may also need a little more cleaning than normal in the bad weather. However, any extra time required here will be amply made up for during the good weather. In this place you will put in the number of times you will clean the entrances and doors. The entrance(s) to your client's offices are very important and he will appreciate your care in these areas.

Washrooms:

Cleaning of the washrooms is also important. Here fill in the proper frequency per week on the outline. Every time you clean the office you will also clean the washrooms. In other words, if you are providing a 5 night a week service, then you will also clean the washrooms 5 nights a week. As mentioned before, keep in mind the absolute importance of always making sure that there is enough toilet tissue and hand towels in each washroom and not forgetting to top up the soap in the dispensers, and deodorant blocks in the urinals. In cleaning the washrooms don't forget to clean the mirror(s) and then polish the chrome taps with a paper towel and a little glass cleaner. You can use the same paper towel that you used to clean the mirror(s).

We have found that if we keep the ladies happy with a clean washroom then everyone is happy. Take special attention to make sure that everything is done well in the ladies washroom: lots of supplies... hand towels, soap, toilet tissue, etc. We have gained contracts because of our competitor's negligence in this area. This is not a hard thing to do. Even though this has been mentioned before, it is good to keep this key point in mind.

Finger marks:

In most professional offices the number of finger marks that need to be removed from the walls etc., is very minimal. Where there are finger marks, a quick wipe with a sponge is all it takes to remove them. We do have a clause in our "Service Outline" that states we will remove finger marks as long as it doesn't change the appearance of the wall. In other words, we will remove finger marks, but the washing of walls is an extra service and is billed as such.

Carpeting:

This is self-explanatory. This generally deals only with regular maintenance of the carpets. Just fill in the frequency of cleaning. Carpets will be vacuumed each time you clean the office whether it is nightly or not.

Floors:

In this section we are referring to the floors that are not carpeted. These are floors like ceramic, terrazzo, or glazed tiles. The reason for the "/" between washed/ spray buffed/waxed is for the sole purpose for you to decide what the floor needs.

The rest is self-explanatory. Just fill in the frequency of cleaning. Usually in a nightly service the floors are just swept and then only spot cleaned if necessary to remove any coffee spills or the like. It is usually understood that in the bad winter weather we include damp mopping the front entrance of our client's office. In a nightly service, the floors (uncarpeted) get completely washed once per week.

If your client is a once or twice a week service then the floors will be completely washed once a week. In the case of a twice a week service, one of the cleaning times will be mid-week and the other will usually be on the weekend. The floors will be washed/waxed/buffed, etc., on the weekend. Some cleaning companies stagger their twice a week services to something like Tuesday and Thursday. In this case the floors will be washed/buffed on the Thursday.

There is absolutely no hard and fast rule for the frequency of cleaning for a twice a week service. Whatever works out for your schedule and fits your client's needs and approval - will work. In our case we always did a twice a week service on Wednesday and the weekends. This way it was always nice and clean for them to come into on Monday.

Regardless of the frequency of cleaning, in our case the more time consuming work such as washing floors and spray buffing was left until the weekend. This would allow us for freedom in scheduling.

Areas to be serviced:

On your first visit with your client you were given a tour of your client's office of which you also took notes. Here in this part of the outline you will specify briefly by naming the areas that you will clean. This is important because it shows the areas serviced and also indirectly indicates the areas that are not included, thus avoiding any confusion later regarding areas your client thought were included in the price. Please see sample outline.

Payment:

This section shows clearly the amount of payment per month. It specifies the amount written out in full and in numbers. It also gives you a continuous outline/agreement if you wish. The outline states that it is automatically renewed from year to year. The only interruption would be that of a price increase, a cancellation from either party or a major change in cleaning requirements.

Do not underestimate the need of this signed outline in your business. If for some reason your client cancels your services he is required to give one month's notice. This will give you time to remedy any problem or simply find another cleaning contract.

Any additional services:

Here this clearly indicates that anything not included in this outline is additional and will be invoiced as such.

Starting Date:

This will be the date that you will start cleaning your client's office.

Company Names:

Your company name will go on the second last line and your client's company name will go on the last line. Each of you must sign the outline to validate it.

VIEWING THE SAMPLES

On the next few pages we have provided samples of the Service Outline, Invoice, and Advertising Letter. Incase the sample views might not be easily read, we have also included below a special link that will enable you to download the samples for easier viewing. Just type the link below into your favorite browser and press enter.

If you would like to download these sample forms to your computer or tablet please use this Google link: https://goo.gl/o2QFK2

If you have any difficulties in downloading the samples, please feel free to contact us so we can arrange for you to have them. You can contact us at: james.revie@gmail.com

The is the front cover for the Service Outline. We print this and the Service Outline on a "parchment" type paper and then cerlox bind it.

Service Outline

especially prepared for

Mr. John Doe
XYZ Company Corporation
789 SomeStreet,
City, State/Province   Zip/PC

Your Cleaning Company
123 Best Street
Best City, Best State/Province Zip/PC
Tel: (123) 456-789   FAX: (321) 654-987

Your Cleaning Company Name

The Janitorial Cleaning Specialists
☐ Commercial   ☐ Industrial

123 Somestreet, Sometown State/Province, Zip/Postal Code
Telephone: (123) 456 - 7890

Service Outline

Especially prepared for
Mr. John Doe
XYZ Company Corporation
789 Goodstreet, City, State, Zip

Cleaning equipment and supplies.	All equipment and supplies will be supplied by our Maintenance Department.
Time of Cleaning.	Services shall be performed between the hours of 6pm - and 7am. so as not to interfere with your business routine.
Note:	This shall be a _____ times a week service.
Duties:	Emptying and damp wiping of ash trays and waste paper baskets and similar receptacles. Dusting of desks, 'phones, furniture, pictures, filing cabinets, etc. Cleaning of counters, tables, drinking fountains, dusting of computers and computer screens.
Waste paper and litter.	Waste paper and ashtrays etc., shall be emptied_____times weekly. Waste paper shall be placed in designated location as specified by you. Ash trays wiped clean and waste paper container liners renewed as required.

Entrances and Entrance glass doors: Glass entrance doors shall be cleaned of finger and soil marks _____ times weekly. Entrance doors shall be thoroughly cleaned weekly.

Finger marks on walls etc. Finger and soil marks (within reason) shall be removed from walls, doors, etc., providing it will not spoil the appearance of the walls etc.

This service outline does not include complete wall washing unless otherwise stated.

Carpeting. Carpets in your premises shall be vacuumed _____ times weekly.

Washrooms Washrooms shall be serviced _____ times weekly. Washrooms supplies to be replenished as required.

Floors. All floors (covered) shall be maintained in the following manner.

Floors shall be swept and dusted _____ times weekly. Floors shall be washed/spray buffed/waxed as required.

Areas to be serviced. Main Office, Side Offices, Boardroom, Computer Room, Lounge, washrooms, entrances.

Payment for all these services shall amount to _____
_____ per month. Payable to (your company name) one month from the starting date and each consecutive month thereafter.

This service outline is in effect for one year from stating date, but may be canceled at any time by either party by giving one month's written notice by registered mail. However, if no notice is given it is automatically renewed from year to year.

    Any additional services shall be invoiced separately.

Starting Date: ....

Your Company Name ....

Your Client's Company Name ....

Your Cleaning Company Name
The Janitorial Cleaning Specialists

☐ Commercial ☐ Industrial ☐ Fully Bonded and Insured

123 Somestreet, Sometown State/Province, Zip/Postal Code
Telephone: (123) 456 - 7890

Invoice

Month Day, Year

XYZ Company Corporation
789 GoodStree,
State,   Zip
days.

Terms: Net 10

Cleaning for the month of January $6,000.00
Two Cases of hand towels ($12 ea)................ $ 24.00

Total: ……………………………………….. $6,024.00

Your Cleaning Company Name
The Janitorial Cleaning Specialists

● Commercial   ● Industrial   ● Fully Bonded and Insured

123 Somestreet, Sometown State/Province, Zip/Postal Code
Telephone: (123) 456 - 7890

> This is a typical advertising letter that we use. It doesn't have to be fancy or wordy. Just state the facts.

Date.

XYZ Company Corporation
123 Somestree,
Somecity, State/Prov   Zip/PC

Att: Mr. John Doe

Dear Mr. John Doe

We would like to thank you for this opportunity of approaching you regarding the cleaning maintenance of your offices.

We are a professional Janitorial Cleaning company who pride ourselves in a job well done and continued customer satisfaction all at a very competitive price.

We would be pleased to give you a free, no obligation estimate on your particular cleaning needs.

If you would like a free, no obligation estimate on your office cleaning needs just give us a call today at 123-456-6789

We are looking forward to hearing from you soon.

Yours truly

Your Name
Your Company Name

33

HOW TO MAKE EVEN MORE MONEY

In this book we have advocated that obtaining easy to clean offices that you can be in and out fast are the best offices to acquire. We have also given you a list of what some of those offices might be.

But in this chapter we would like to explain to you the principal of "Diversification." Someone has rightly said that diversification is the key. This is true in the cleaning business as well.

When you have a healthy Office Cleaning Business this will open many possible doors of diversification that can result in some very good financial benefits. Because you will have an established relationship with managers, executives and other decision makers you can then offer them other services that you are interested in providing for them.

Here is a sample list for you to consider:

- Carpet Cleaning
- Window Cleaning
- Snow Removal

- Wall Washing
- Ceiling Tile Replacement (suspended type ceiling tiles)
- Window Blind Cleaning
- Computer Keyboard Deep Cleaning
- Entrance Walk Way Matt Provider (you get a %)
- Office Moving
- Factory/Warehouse Floor Sweeping - requires dust control product
- Grass Cutting and various Lawn Care Services
- Residential (Home) Cleaning
- Sidewalk, Driveway Power Washing
- Outside Building Power Washing
- Painting and Decorating Services (consulting and or doing it)
- Restoration Services - requires additional training and equipment

Actually the list could go on and on. The point is this - whatever service your client would pay someone else to do, if you can do it, why not go for it. Becoming diversified should be easy because you have a trusted relationship already with your current client. This is a great way to increase you income and thus make for money monthly.

When we were on the West Coast running our two successful cleaning business we did not need to diversify or go after additional work as listed above, but we did have one major client that came to us and asked if we could do a number of the things list above. We did and as a result our monthly income grew even larger.

If you desire to diversify, I would suggest you consider getting your main cleaning business up and running first. After that you could diversify and see how it goes. Just a thought for you to consider.

34

CONCLUSION

We have covered a lot of material in this book. But I believe that it is material that will help you in many ways. If you purchased the special Boxed Set Bundled Package there will be more information and resources for you in the books/sections to follow.

I would recommend that you go through the various chapters within this book again until you feel really comfortable that you understand the concepts and ideas behind what is being said. Our hope is that you are successful on the first try.

If you have enjoyed this book it would be a "tremendous" help if you could leave a review so others will know that it has been helpful to you.

In addition, we would love to hear of your success. Please email us and let us know how it went/is going for you and your business. You can email us at the same email address above.

To your success

James Revie - Author

www.ingramcontent.com/pod-product-compliance
Lightning Source LLC
Chambersburg PA
CBHW071505220526
45472CB00003B/920